Impactful Instructional Leadership
&
Framework for Success

- FRAMEWORK FOR SUCCESS -

Instructional Leaders must ensure they share what their idea of impact is and what they believe educators can accomplish. Are your educators better because they have you as their Instructional Leader? Do you have high expectations for all educators or only the educators who put forth the greatest effort? We must have high expectations for all educators in the school. Perceptions must change and vigor must be applied to all.

To Reach Principal Hunter
www.masterybasedlearning.com
Facebook.com/principalhunterofficial
Email:principalJhunter@gmail.com
Twitter:@principaljack

Table of Contents

How This Book Is Organized

This book is organized into six chapters. Chapter One will start your move forward into becoming an Instructional Leader aiming for your own personal vision of success for you and your organization. Chapter Two defines all the characteristics and qualities that are needed to have a meaningful impact on your organization by your leadership qualities. Chapter Three explains Shared Leadership and the importance of impactful collaboration. Chapter Four, the Instructional Leader, acts as the Data Warrior and uses data to put practices into action. Chapter Five is developing coherence between Instructional Leader and school staff through a Coaching Model and process. Chapter Six is explained in detail as the articulation of successful Evidence-Based practices.

Throughout this publication, you will read about Evidence-Based practices. *Evidence-Based practices* are defined as "effective educational strategies supported by evidence and research." When teachers use evidence-based practices with fidelity, they can be confident their teaching will support student learning and achievement. Evidence-Based practices are paramount for educators to understand and implement if you are going to be an impactful Instructional Leader.

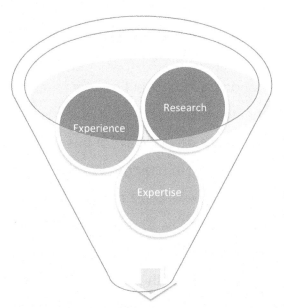

Evidence-Based Practices

Research: Academic finding and meta-analysis.

Expertise: Calculating effect size and validating meta-analysis studies for your school.

Experience: What works? Share best practices.

On a final note on how the book is organized, you will notice a puzzle piece or pieces at the beginning of each chapter. After finishing this book, you will have completed the puzzle and be on track to implement your vision as an Instructional Leader.

Preface

The first realization Instructional Leaders must understand is that the goal is not to change people; it is to move thinking toward emulating the vision or "Why" of the organization. As leaders, we must be open to change. We are responsible for making the changes in the organization. Instructional Leadership is measured daily. The 16 action steps from the puzzle are a culmination of strategies you will use to be successful over the course of the forthcoming years. You will notice at the beginning of each chapter which action step(s) are focused on in each chapter. Instructional Leadership is not a culmination of initiatives you have been successful with over the course of years. Consider Instructional Leadership your formative assessment.

If we assess, reflect and revaluate our actions, the summative results will embody the hard work and dedication we do daily. I can unequivocally guarantee, if you follow these processes throughout the book, you will become a more impactful Instructional Leader and your school will become a more vibrant, positive, learning environment. When you think about Instructional Leadership, what comes to your mind? Is it coaching teachers, visiting classrooms, picking out and implementing new curriculum or modeling best practices? If you selected any or all of the above, you are moving in the right direction in your journey.

It is imperative that you understand what good leadership practice looks like, sounds like and how to drive educators to be catalysts for your change. As a leadership coach, remind yourself, "Every day, leaders must wake up and lead themselves before they lead anyone else. Other people are depending on you; you must keep the fire burning within yourself. You must know where your organization is going (Vision), know why they are going in that direction (Shared Leadership/Using Evidence-Based Practices), and help all others to get there (Coaching/Reflection)." Are you ready to begin your journey to discovering your "Why" both for yourself and your organization? Are you ready to spend time learning about yourself, your strengths and your vision as they relate to Instructional Leadership? One of the most identified qualities of great leaders is a clear vision!

Introduction

On July 18, 1918, born was a human who would change the lives of millions of fellow countryman and the views of millions of others. Apartheid was rampant in South Africa and in many minds would still continue if it was not for the life of one man and a movement. Could you imagine spending 27 years in prison for a cause you know is right and sacrificing your freedom to keep it in the forefront? How about refusing to believe the archaic views of the leaders of the country and not only be imprisoned, but spend the time smashing large rocks into small rocks as a punishment? While in prison, being the leader he was, he collaborated with eight other prisoners on when they would be released and how they intended to end Apartheid in South Africa. Even then, while imprisoned, he found the need to collaborate and use his leadership skills to start a movement. This of course is the story of Nelson Mandela. Imprisoned with a continual vision for an Apartheid free South Africa, Mandela quickly rose to the ranks of government once he was released from prison in 1982. The current leadership of South Africa, when Mandela was released, agreed that Apartheid was against humanity and allowed Mandela to solicit the consensus to live out his vision. Mandela went on to earn the Nobel Peace Prize and serve his countrymen and women for years, ensuring equity amongst all. He started with a vision and knew the hard work and steadfast commitment that was needed to ensure the people he served were able to reach their true potential. Nelson Mandela, in my opinion, is a true hero of people and a leader we all should look to emulate.

So, why do I retell the story of Nelson Mandela in an Educational Leadership book? The point this story conveys is that even in the harshest of conditions, having a clear vision and "Why" of your role can assist you with overcoming immense obstacles. Mandela overcame and ended Apartheid. We, as Instructional Leaders, are tasked with improving student achievement, preparing learners for college and career readiness, and ensuring their social emotional needs are met. With a clear vision, that goal is within reach.

The Components of Instructional Leadership

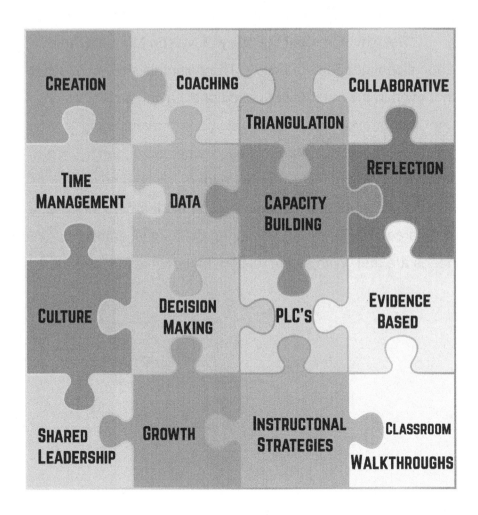

All these pieces fit together to complete the Instructional Leadership Puzzle

Chapter 1

Creating Vision & Framework for Success

Create and Communicate the Vision of Excellence Using Success Criteria

The vision of an organization is the starting point and driving force behind the creation of a positive culture. An educationally focused culture will yield a clear vision and defined expectations (Success Criteria). Having a clear vision is an excellent way to hold you accountable as an Instructional Leader. Throughout this chapter, there will be a process for you to follow to create an Instructional Leadership vision statement for you, as the leader. Your personal vision reflects your current and future aspirations toward being an exceptional Instructional Leader.

A true vision determines your purpose as an Instructional leader. It is used as a guide to assist, make decisions, which provides direction, and describes what you want to achieve in the future.

Many organizations lose focus of their vision, which causes unsuccessful results. You will read an example of an educational correlation and a business correlation, so you can understand the validity and importance of a solid vision statement. An educational example would be the lack of growth mindset. In previous decades, educators believed that what students did and could do predicted what they could accomplish. Previous educators were not provided the growth mindset research that proved when students were taught using different modalities and strategies to solve problems, they were likely to improve. Carol Dweck states a fixed mindset consists of educators believing that students' brains were not elastic and students have already pre-determined intellect. This fixed mindset allowed schools to focus on what they were doing, rather than focusing on improving each learner to their maximum potential. Furthermore, they weren't tasked with educating all styles and skill levels of learners. In most schools today, this fixed mindset is extinct and educators believe that all students can learn and have the ability to improve (Growth Mindset).

An example in business of Carol Dweck's fixed mindset would be Sears Department Store. Sears was a staple in communities for decades with their unbreakable craftsman tools and massive catalogs. However, Sears did not embrace the suburban sprawl and technology. As a result, they were left with ill-equipped real estate locations and items that were not as desirable as their competitors' current contents. Sears forgot the vision of what it means to be a leader in department store merchandise or home improvement. The company eventually had to close stores and sell off its most profitable brands to stay afloat for a period of time. Instead of rebranding or understanding their vision of why they were successful, they continued to focus on what they did previously. Unfortunately, Sears suffered demise.

Granted, you can become a successful manager while also being efficient at how things are completed, but you won't transform your organization without a clear vision of "why you exist as a school". Most school leaders are tasked with all the technical demands of management and then asked to drive instruction through Data, PLCs and Professional Learning. In the next few chapters, I will provide more examples and resources on how to navigate the technical demands of the job, while still empowering you to lead your school's vision as an Instructional Leader.

As I am working with other leaders, I refer to this short read, *Yertle the Turtle* by Dr. Seuss. It is important to remember to be humble and realize that everyone in the organization is looking at you to lead them. The leader's job in an educational organization, or any other organization, is to provide its employees with a feeling of self-worth, agency and connection. This book emulates what leaders often do in struggling organizations or schools that lose focus of their vision.

Here is a short recap and the leadership lesson that is so vital:

"Yertle the Turtle" by Dr. Seuss:

"...Yertle, the king of them all, decided the kingdom he ruled was too small. "I'm ruler," said Yertle, "of all that I see. But I don't see enough. That's the trouble with me."
So Yertle, the Turtle King, lifted his hand and Yertle, the Turtle King, gave a command. He ordered nine turtles to swim to his stone and, using these turtles, he built a new throne."

The nine turtles are consistent with an individual who is climbing the corporate ladder. Yertle the Turtle is not content with just being a leader. He must step on and use every turtle to make himself feel he is in charge, definitely not a servant mindset. Instructional Leaders need a mindset of which each individual adds value to the organization. In this story, however, it shows an opposite mindset where the only person in charge has value and the others' role is to provide the platform for the leader's success. By not developing the turtles around him, his organization will be stymied and his kingdom will never achieve his desired aspirations.

To further explain, Instructional Leaders must realize that the goal is not to change people; but to move thinking toward emulating the vision or "Why" of the organization!

Growth Area #1: Instructional Leadership: Create Your Personal Vision or "Why" Statement

The first part of your personal vision or "Why" statement should be the contribution you make to the lives of others. It should be granular enough that it relates to your current position, but also broad enough to cover all aspects of your role.

The second part of your personal vision or "Why" statement should be the impact your contribution has on the stakeholders and its surrounding community. In this section, think a bit more broadly. What do you envision the community, staff, students and stakeholders to experience when you have evolved as an Instructional Leader? Where do you envision the greatest impact of your vision?

Here is an example of my current "Why" statement that I have used for the past seven years.

My "Why" Statement: "To develop significant leaders so they can change the world by uncovering the human talent around them". This is the personal leadership vision that I created and shared with my organization. My statement embodies what I do as an Instructional Leader every day. I can also be accountable by reflecting daily on how my actions relate back to my personal leadership vision.

Creation of Your Instructional Leadership Vision "Why" Statement:

Now is the time to begin and create your personal vision statement. As you begin to craft your vision statement, think back to each puzzle piece and how it relates to your current perception of you, as an Instructional Leader. What are some of the qualities that inspire you to change? Where do you see immense growth with applied effort? Do you lead with a growth mindset? What persuades you to change your current practices?

_____

_____

_____

Remember your personal vision statement can be revised and refined as your view of yourself as an Instructional Leader changes with growth and development.

Growth Area #2: Lead Staff in Development of Their Personal Vision or "Why" Statements

Once completed, it is now time to reveal your personal vision statement and explain your thought processes and relevance to staff, students and community. As you begin to assist your staff crafting their "Why" statements, remember that humans have an innate desire to belong to a cause or vision. As teachers are creating their statements, it should be a belief. Their actions should emulate their educational convictions.

This may seem more like a philosophy exercise than an educational one. Trust me though, no one wants to follow or be empowered by a leader who does not have a succinct purpose.

Instructional Leader Prerequisite Prior to Implementing with Staff:

Before I present new ideas, strategies, or desired changes to educators, I always ensure it is Evidence-Based. It is imperative that as an Instructional Leader, you only model for staff ideas or practices that are vetted and deemed *research* or *Evidence-Based*.

John Hattie's number one strategy for instructional improvement is Teacher Collective Efficacy. He goes on to explain and define *teacher efficacy* as "...Collective Teacher Efficacy is the collective belief of teachers in their ability to positively affect students." With an effect size of d=1.57, Collective Teacher Efficacy is strongly correlated with student achievement. Strong collective efficacy encourages individual teachers to make effective use of the skills they already have. Strong collective efficacy allows teams to function productively. While you are introducing the impact of collective efficacy to your entire staff, it is important to model and show staff how you created your own vision statement. It is important as you are developing this practice with your staff they understand that their individual teacher efficacy will assist the organization with improvement. The vision statement is the reminder of what their "Why" is for coming to work each day.

Step 1: Share your personal vision or "Why" statement with staff. I would recommend you post your statement so the entire staff is able to view it. Break down each phrase or thought. Explain how you derived each part and the significance it has on the organization. This is the first step in beginning to show your staff you are willing to complete every activity you ask them to complete. It reveals that you carefully planned out the exercise, modeled it and provided your own example to make it personal. In future chapters, this "modeling/coaching" will be a vital part of your transformation as an Instructional Leader.

Step 2: Provide the remainder of the time for staff to create their personal vision or "Why" statement. If more time is needed, provide it during staff meetings or other contracted time.

An example of incorporating and presenting steps 1 & 2 to your staff is as follows:

Introduction: Today we will be working as a staff to craft your own personal "Why" vision statement. These statements will be developed to understand what inspires you to be the best educator or employee you can be. Some things I would like you to think about when working on your "Why" statements are as follows:
1. **Has to be actionable**
2. **Must be clear, easy to read and to understand**
3. **Must effect change or help others**
4. **Must use affirmative language that resonates with you**

Simon Sinek, in his book *"Discover Your Why"*, uses this great format that may help you develop your personal vision statement:

TO_____SO THAT_____.

The first part should be the contribution the author makes to the lives of others. The second part should be the impact your contribution has on the organization or people you are serving. Keep in mind we are not products or services. As you reflect daily, this statement should help drive your decisions and your self-reflection. When staff members finally create their "Why" statements, they need time to reflect at staff meetings. Once that vision or "Why" statement is casted and is placed outside the doors of educators, the school has the bottom layer of foundation completed.

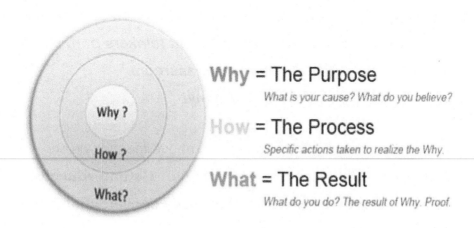

Why = The Purpose
What is your cause? What do you believe?

How = The Process
Specific actions taken to realize the Why.

What = The Result
What do you do? The result of Why. Proof.

Here are a few examples created by current staff members:

"To motivate, support, and encourage all learners to achieve their maximum potential by providing a safe environment with high expectations academically, socially, and emotionally thus building a foundation for lifelong learning."
-Mrs. Grohnke

"To empower students to become motivated, responsible, lifelong learners through fun and engaging experiences."
-Mr. Cowell

"To create a classroom that stimulates the mind, fosters compassion, and inspires learners to stretch themselves so that they can become independent thinkers both inside and outside of the classroom."
-Mrs. Urbanyi

It is perfectly fine to share the above teacher vision statements with your staff as a guideline. **Getting educators to think about their vision will produce conversations that will impact student achievement.**

Crafting Your School Vision or "Why" Statement

When you think about a school having a vision, you think about harmony of vision. Unity is truly about maximizing uniqueness and channeling that toward the common goals of the organization. Your district may have a mission and vision statement, as most do, and some schools already have a school-based mission statement. It is just as important to have a school vision statement! What is the criterion for a student to be deemed successful at the end of the year? Educators must clearly define and be able to articulate what success looks like for all learners. The school vision statement should be representative of your community and its needs. Most of the school vision statements I have read are very vague or were crafted many years ago. Here's an example of one in which many deem as a great vision statement:

"The vision of (schools name), a diverse and growing community of unique individuals, is to ensure that each child will experience optimal social, emotional, academic and physical success through a challenging and progressive child-centered educational program in a safe and healthy learning environment." For an overview, it has all the buzzwords but no call to action. There are too many actions that need to be explained and assessed for an educator or learner to be successful. It is important when crafting a school vision statement that you are able to articulate easily what the student learning profile should look like after a successful year. If you recently completed a vision statement, revisit it to make sure everyone truly understands the "What" and "How" of embodying the school vision. I like to have the school vision or "Why" statement of the school read on the morning announcements, as well. Additionally, empowering students and educators to recite it and understand what it means as a classroom everyday can be powerful. I also encourage school educators to share their personal vision statement that is posted outside their door with their students frequently.

Now, on a daily basis, find a way to convey to your staff that the students and educators are a part of a great school with a positive effect on students every day. I do this daily by reading a few positive referrals on the afternoon announcements. Educators submit names of students who exceeded expectations either behaviorally, academically or socially and they place them in a basket by my office. I then read the names over the afternoon announcements. Learners love hearing their names in a positive light. I normally will provide a pencil or other trinket when their name is called. Another way we emulate positivity is by celebrating growth on our quarterly assessments. Anyone who shows growth of 7% or more gets to run down the music-filled hallways while students and educators cheer for them.

As we look at the different groups of people that can help move your vision forward, you must also look to all staff members in your building and other staff members who embody your vision, as well.

I will leave you with one final quote to help you create your vision. Pete Carroll, Head Coach of the Seattle Seahawks, states, "If you create a vision for yourself and stick with it, you can make amazing things happen in your life. Once you have done the work to create the clear vision it is the discipline and effort to maintain that vision, which can make it all, come true."

Summary

"A great leader's courage to fulfil his vision comes from passion, not position." by John Maxwell. After creating your personal vision statement, assisting staff members in creating their own personal vision statement and creating your school vision statement, you should feel empowered to lead. Continue to revisit and review your vision or "Why" information. Your vision statement will help you remain focused through the trial and tribulations as an Instructional Leader. There will be days where you feel you cannot be the Instructional Leader you want to be. On those days, it is extra important to read and re-read your personal vision statement in order to endure the bumps in the road to achieve all the successful days ahead.

As Simon Sinek states in "*Starts with Why*: "Leading is not the same as being a leader." Being a leader means you hold the highest rank, either by earning it, having good fortune or navigating internal politics. "Leading, however, means that others willingly follow you; not because they have to, not because they are paid to, but because they want to."

Jim Rohn the Master of Influence states, "The most important investment you and I will ever make is in ourselves. That investment will determine the return that we get out of life." He further goes on to state, "Learn to work harder on yourself than you do your job." Self-reflection is the catalyst that clearly embodies this. If I wanted my school to outperform previous years, I knew I had to improve as a leader and it had to start with a clear vision.

Change really isn't as hard as we thought if we capture people's interest and give them enjoyable, worthwhile experiences.

--Michael Fullan

Leadership is about setting a direction. It's about creating a vision, empowering and inspiring people to want to achieve the vision, and enabling them to do so with energy and speed through an effective strategy. In its most basic sense, leadership is about mobilizing a group of people to jump into a better future.

--John P. Kotter

Chapter 2

Instructional Leadership

"**Understand that the Impact you have on one educator can cause a positive wave of change in your organization.**"
--Jack Hunter

Now that you have your vision or "Why", I would like you to take a few minutes to think about what Instructional Leadership means to you and how you would define it.

Define: Instructional Leadership is:

_____

_____

_____

_____

If you were like me, you googled Instructional Leadership and found 30+ different definitions. And that's just it; it is extremely subjective. I continually research leadership trends and Evidence-Based practices to ensure my understanding of Instructional Leadership is current and relevant. This reminds the readers that Instructional Leaders need to develop their own guiding vision and philosophy. It must be evidence and research-based and pertain to you personally in order to be portrayed authentically to all stakeholders. Over the years, as a principal, I have mentored other leaders on the importance of developing their own definition of Instructional Leadership and staying relevant with all new educational trends and research. I define Instructional Leadership for my staff as:

Hunter defined it as: A collaborative partnership between the lead learner and educators that allows for fluid collaboration around student data, equity, diversity and has an impact on curriculum, assessment, student growth and proficiency.

Here are some examples of definitions of Educational Leadership that I have correlated and provided for you to reflect upon. Use this time to reflect on your definition and adjust it as it fits you and your organization.

"Instructional Leadership involves setting clear goals, managing curriculum, monitoring lesson plans, allocating resources and evaluating teachers regularly to promote student learning and growth." unknown

"Instructional Leadership in education places focus on learning for children and adults alike. It particularly focuses on learning that can be measured by development in instruction and in the distinction of student learning." Teamworkdefiniton.com.

"An Educational Leader serves as a guide and influences other educators in an administrative setting." study.com.

"Good Instructional Leadership ensures that educational programs make the desired impact. An effective leader inspires action and takes an optimistic view of the future. They also set a good example by being honest, having integrity and treating people fairly." chron.com.

"Educational leadership is the process of enlisting and guiding the talents and energies of teachers, pupils, and parents toward achieving common educational aims." Open source

"Educational Leadership is usually the responsibility of school administrators and principals, who strive to create positive change in educational policy and processes." learn.org.

"In short, Instructional Leadership reflects those actions a principal takes to promote growth in student-learning (Flath, 1989). The Instructional Leader makes instructional quality the top priority of the school and attempts to bring that vision to realization." NAESP.

Optional Activity If you find yourself influenced by one of the above quotes, now is the time to reflect and refine your Instructional Leadership vision statement.

Reflect and refine on original definition of Instructional Leadership.

_____

_____

_____

_____

"What you value is what you will find time for."

--John Maxwell

Reflection is defined as a mental process. It is an interpretation of what is going on between learning and thinking. Reflection is also an opportunity to gain self-knowledge and raise self-awareness.

Time to take a pretest and reflect on your Instructional Leadership Readiness!

While taking this pre-assessment, please rate yourself on a scale of 1 to 3, with 3 computing the statement as a strength.

1= area of weaknesses

2= area of refinement

3= area of reinforcement

Number	Self-Assessment Conceptual Ideas	Rating (1,2,3) 3-Highest
1.1	I ensure that curriculum, instruction and assessments are aligned to maximize student learning.	
1.2	I am confident that I improve classroom teaching by observing, coaching and evaluating all faculty and staff.	
1.3	I use data to move beyond problem identification to **problem solving.**	
1.4	I can gather **additional data** to better understand causes related to problems in question.	
1.5	I **promote** and encourage innovative and creative teacher practice.	
1.6	I **ensure** assessments are reliable and valid for my students.	

1.7	I monitor and **track** the use of formative assessments of student progress at regular intervals throughout the year.	
1.8	I model and provide support to ensure the use of digital age tools enrich the instructional learning for all.	
1.9	I identify strategies for building a sense of efficacy and empowerment among staff.	
2.0	**I monitor and track** the use of data to make decisions about professional development plans.	
2.1	I mentor and support the development of all faculty and staff.	
2.2	I use **data in conversations** with parents about student performance and future goals.	
2.3	I create a flexible and reliable learning environment, free of distractions.	
2.4	I monitor and track data though the use of data walls or data notebooks, ensuring equity in data collection and assessment.	
	Total	

Now that you have taken the self-assessment and collated your totals, you are ready to reflect on the results. It is important that you understand your strengths. Continue to develop those strengths as you grow as an Instructional Leader. This assessment is an organic document that can be referred to yearly, or as needed, but at a minimum, every year. This will ensure your Instructional Leadership skills continue to be measured via self-assessment. This document can also be revisited mid-year as a checks and balances system for your goal planning.

Questions:

Which two areas did you rate yourself the highest in and why?

Item #_____

Why:

_____

_____

_____

_____

Item #_____
Why:

_____

_____

_____

_____

Which area did you rate yourself as needing the most development in and why?

Item#_____
Why:

_____

_____

_____

_____

As you continue to progress as an Instructional Leader, the forthcoming chapters (Data and Coaching) will provide numerous ideas and strategies to assist you with your improvement in the areas that need the most development. You will also be challenged to implement new practices in the areas where you rate yourself above average or measured a score of 3. These new strategies to implement are included in chapters three, four and five..

A great example of a person who overcame his obstacles, understood his strengths, and worked on his weaknesses, is Olympic swimmer, Michael Phelps. Michael was diagnosed with ADHD at an early age and struggled in school immensely. That all changed when he discovered the pool. Michael was able to assess himself both before and after he swam in order to work on the areas he needed to refine. Self-assessment is a necessary tool as an Instructional Leader to ensure you are aligned to your vision, the vision of the school and to the vision of your school district.

Communicating Within and Across the Organization

Remember that communication is not all verbal. In fact, it is a small part of how you are perceived. When attending an American Management Association Training on Communication, they stated that *impact on conversation* is as follows:

Words 7%

Vocal Tone 38%

Body Language 55%

This amazed me! I wanted to see it for myself. I stood in front of the mirror and began to have a mock conversation. The results were less than positive. When I spoke, I watched my eyes and my body signals. I noticed that I had slight negative body language at times and needed to be more conscious of these movements and expressions to ensure I was able to provide a safe, risk-free conversation with stakeholders. Practice being on the other side of yourself! It will amaze you how people perceive you. If you need other help, ask a trusted co-worker, family member or a critical friend for suggestions. It is imperative as an aspiring leader and seasoned veteran to continue to watch your communication traits as you work with a variety of people throughout your tenure.

Communication as an Instructional Leader is ultra-important as you ask educators and staff members to transform their practice. Here are some things to remember on your posture:

1. Keep your spine tall and strong.
2. Stand with weight balanced equally on both feet. DO NOT SWAY.
3. Keep your head level.
4. Point your nose to the listener.
5. Command the space around you.

The number one distraction speakers make when presenting is swaying.

Here are some specific strategies that should be practiced when speaking. Make sure you attempt these in front of a mirror first:

1. Move no more than once every 45-60 seconds or when you progress to a new idea in a presentation.
2. Whenever you do move, remain still until you meet the criteria in step one. Watching someone who is constantly moving while presenting is distracting and tiring for the observer.
3. Keep your posture open to the entire audience, not just half of the room.

4. Keep your head up while moving. Looking down or away causes your audience to lose focus on you as the presenter.

The second most common distraction is the flailing of hands as people are presenting.

This is common and causes the observer to watch the hands instead of listening to the content of the speaker's program. I want to address some skills to practice to ensure you are not speaking wholly with your hands. Note: your communication style can include your hands, but just being observant of where they move during your presentation can result in a less distracted audience.

Hand movement is mostly a subconscious behavior and you must train yourself to keep your hands in your gesture box. This "area" of the body is equivalent to your waistline to mid chest. All activity with your hands other than an occasional chop (a swift movement from your head to waist) or power movement should occur in your gesture box. This will ensure the listener is looking at you as you are speaking and not at your hands flailing around while trying to command your space.

These strategies should become a part of your communication style while interacting with all staff members, educators, community members, students and parents. It is important that you model correct communication styles to allow your staff to respond to you as the Instructional Leader.

As a leader, when speaking, it is important to have strong vocal and visual skills. Some ideas from an amazing book *"The Credibility Code"* by Cara Alter, are as follows:

1. Ensure your volume is full and consistent with clear articulation.
2. Pacing is relaxed and appears well-rehearsed.
3. Expression is used correctly and highlighted within your message.
4. Eye contact is held for no more than 5 seconds per person.
5. As you are speaking to an individual, ensure your eyes, hands and face are interacting with him/her.

If you continue to implement the above communication traits and practices, you will notice a more attentive audience and you will feel more confident in your ability to speak as an Instructional Leader.

Time Management Activity

Materials Needed:

Post-it Notes
Whiteboard
Pen/Marker

1. For one entire week, write down each activity or task you complete on a separate Post-it-Note. This should include, but not be limited to, the following: i.e., complete purchase orders/ pick up lunch count/ put items in mailboxes/make copies/classroom visits/meet with parents/ etc. When you complete a Post-it-Note move to step two. Follow this process for an entire week.

2. As you complete each task, place them on your whiteboard that is divided into:
   Keep Doing   *Stop Doing*   *Delegate Doing*

The next step is to either leave the above items on your whiteboard or copy them into a notebook if privacy is an issue. This activity of *keep doing, stop doing, delegate doing* should continue to take place with

monthly reflection. As you reflect on the decisions you are making daily, ensure you are looking at the leadership puzzle to guarantee the time you are spending at school is instructionally based and not consumed with making low-level decisions that do not impact student achievement.

In the next three months, revisit this Time Management Activity and update either the whiteboard or the notebook to assess your growth in these areas. Have you noticed that you have found extra time now in your day that is not consumed by non-instructional items? Continue the *keep doing, stop doing, delegate doing* process if you are struggling with creating open time for student achievement. If you are struggling with time, focus on just one *stop doing* and *delegate doing*. Chapter Three will provide you with ideas to free your time from low- level decisions.

While visiting many principals across the adjoining states and mentoring on Instructional Leadership, one commonality I found was principals stated they were extremely busy and they never had time to be Instructional Leaders. This was always at the forefront of our discussions and the reason I created the Time Management Activity. I reminded leaders of the statement **"activity is not accomplishment."** When we discussed this statement, we delved into what takes up their time as a leader. It is extremely easy throughout the day to be majoring in minor details. I like to call this "majoring in the minors". While we are still tasked with running school operations, we must focus on the delegating piece to ensure our time is not consumed with items that do not improve student achievement. Throughout research, I have found that the top skill needed for time management is the ability to successfully delegate. Learning to delegate will assist Instructional Leaders to produce a positive school culture as you are viewed as a leader who is not authoritarian. Chapter Three on Shared Leadership will give you a plethora of ideas and strategies as you move forward.

Improving Academic Culture

I feel it is extremely important to discuss how to improve and evaluate the Academic Culture of your building as you work on implementing vision statements and hone your Instructional Leadership skills. You must work and create a culture that is effective in producing great outcomes. Some of the key ideas that you must ensure occur when working with your educators are as follows:

1. Ensure you are honest and transparent in your thoughts with your staff and expect the same from them. The great basketball player, Michael Jordan,

stated, "Mistakes are like those little puzzles that, when you solve them, they give you a gem. Every mistake that you make and learn from will save you from thousands of similar mistakes in the future." By following this quote and believing in this mindset ensures that you are a mistake-friendly leader. You ensure when mistakes are corrected, they become part of your school's best practices. One of the statements I like to share with my staff is, *"**Realize that you have nothing to fear from knowing the truth.**"*

2. Have thoughtful disagreements when you believe improvement is needed.

3. Create an agreed upon way of handling disagreement with your staff to ensure stalemates and compromises do not occur (Conflict Resolution Skills).

4. **Never say anything about someone that you wouldn't say to them directly.** I see numerous leaders make this mistake when they confer with others negatively about individuals in the organization. The person you confide in may agree with you, but be assured they will trust you a bit less. They will wonder if you speak about them with others. Be transparent and communicate as if the person you are speaking

about is in front of you. This is a huge catalyst for a positive and ongoing, authentic culture.

All of the above will create an academic culture where all stakeholders interact, make decisions and influence others. **Understand who has potential to be a leader in your staff!**

Collaboration

Collaboration of staff and stakeholders is paramount as you focus on improving yourself as an Instructional Leader. There are numerous ways to collaborate, and in Chapter three, you will focus on sharing leadership and decision-making. But before we delve into sharing the leadership, I want to provide some scaffolds on how important being an Instructional Leader is in the collaboration process. Numerous studies have taken place over the past fifteen years on culture and I can summarize my readings and reports to the following: If the leader creates conditions that allow educators inside the organization to feel safe among each other, they will work together to choose things none of them could have ever achieved alone. When you make this happen, your organization will tower over others.

Furthermore, this does not imply that you praise everyone and don't hold people accountable. It is actually the contrary. According to a 2013 Gallup Poll called, *"The State of the American Workplace"*, the following was proven from the results:

1. When supervisors completely ignore employee work or conversations, 40% of the employees surveyed disengage from their work.

2. When supervisors criticize employees on a regular basis, 22% of employees surveyed actively disengage.

3. When a supervisor recognizes a single strength of the employee and rewards the employee, only 1% will disengage from their work.

Humans have an innate desire to be part of a group. Sure there are exceptions, but research has proven that being a part of a positive group can increase happiness. This proves collaboration is at the heart of all we do.

There are five main principals of collaboration and they are as follows:

1. Applying Trust
2. Respect
3. Willingness
4. Empowerment
5. Effective Communication

Each chapter in this book further reiterates these five principles and how to build them into your daily vision plan for complete school success for all stakeholders.

Collaboration also makes all meetings more productive with flexibility and engaged staff. You, as the Instructional Leader, have built this environment with your collaborative vision statement which lives each day at your school. Collaboration brings all staff together with a shared purpose.

Researching True Collaboration, as the synergistic relationship, forms when two or more entities work toward the results and not the process. Instructional Leadership focuses on the impactful results of collaboration. To achieve these impactful results, the processes are just as important and necessary to achieve successful collaborative results.

Summary

I am asked quite often by leaders and educators if leaders can be made. The simple answer is "Yes. Leadership is developed, not discovered." To further explain, everyone has leadership potential that is undiscovered or undeveloped. This, by no means, insinuates that everyone can be a CEO of a company. It implies that we all have innate traits that can be honed in on and developed to be leaders. It starts with being the best version of you.

As you read and utilize the ideas and proven strategies in this book, you will continue to look at the steps needed to develop your leadership skills and work toward becoming an Instructional Leader. You have undiscovered talent! What you do to develop these Instructional Leadership skills is up to you! Let's begin! The Instructional Leadership process requires a lot of hard work, grit and a servant mindset toward others. Always remember that great leaders don't start out great. It is a process.

Chapter 3

Shared Leadership

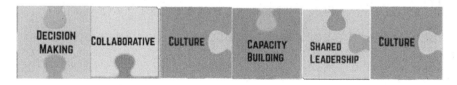

"It's not how we behave during exceptional days, it's how we behave every day that shows our character" --Drew Dudley

"I just want to be right—I don't care if the right answer comes from me."
— Ray Dalio

Shared Leadership has generated a great deal of buzz in educational fields over the past few years as a practice that is impactful for schools. My definition of *Shared Leadership* is *"the sharing of decisions that affect teacher work conditions, culture of the school, community engagements, and professional learning for staff while also encompassing the shared distribution of leadership."* Coming from the business world, Shared Leadership reflects the word "delegate." Thus, sharing the leadership and responsibilities of an educational organization goes far beyond "delegate." Shared Leadership includes decisions that are essential to day-to-day operations.

Why am I more qualified than other people in my organization just because I have a title? Does it really matter where the extra paper is stored or who posts the potluck signup sheet? Are these things what you want to consume your day? It sounds comical. However, when I work with leaders, they are sometimes consumed with low-level decision-making that could be delegated to other people in the building. I empower my leadership team (defined in this chapter) to generate a process for these low-level decisions, and unless it affects students, I am silent in the decisions.

When it comes to instructional items, including all curriculum, I never make a decision without first discussing it with my leadership team. This type of relationship ensures that educators do not change whole curricula or try practices that are not proven through evidence or research before talking with me and the leadership team. Professional Learning Communities, Coaching, and Data are pivotal pieces of the Shared Leadership Puzzle.

I will share with you the Decision Making Protocol I use when making decision processes in an organization. Since you have recently completed the **keep doing, stop doing, delegate doing** process task in the previous chapter, it is a great time to look at items you do daily that could fit into the Shared Leadership model. I studied numerous businesses and other enterprises and decided to focus on the way the Japanese automaker created leadership in their organization.

It has been studied and copied numerous times in society today, and it fits succinctly with the type of leadership I was working toward. The Japanese model simply allows anyone with an idea they believe will help the organization, to present the idea to a member of leadership. A great book to study is, "Gung Ho" by Ken Blanchard. It is a manageable yet extremely effective way to use the author's ideas to help with implementation of sharing of ideas. This simple, straightforward approach toward sharing leadership responsibilities builds trust and focuses and improves positive culture. This is a must read as a book study for you and your staff!

Hunter's Shared Leadership definition (Pg. 51) and style has proven very effective for our school environment and surrounding community. It incorporates the Evidence-Based research of John Hattie. The following Evidence-Based meta-analysis was conducted, validating the Shared Leadership process. The first part of the research was the effect teacher job satisfaction had on the organization d=.71. The second part of the research was transformational approach of Leadership, encouraging teacher growth. This had an effect size of d=.48. There are numerous studies completed on Shared Leadership; however, this was enough for me to validate Shared Leadership as the paradigm for my current school. Shared Leadership creates enhanced relationships with co-workers and a positive culture of trust in addition to, as stated in the Gallup poll, more engagement in the workplace. One of the strengths of Shared Leadership is having an elected teacher leader or union representative serve as the speaker for the educators. Having the individual elected by the teachers at large ensures fairness and fidelity in selection. This position, in my opinion, should be elected by the entire educator body and not appointed by the principal. Here are the steps you need to create and implement a Shared Leadership model in your building.

Leadership Team Creation Process

Step 1: Selection of Leadership Team: There are various ways that a leadership team can be created depending on your collective bargaining agreement, lack of an agreement, or current structure of your school or district. In my experience, successful leadership teams consist of no more than seven members, and the current union or teacher leader must be a member of the team. In addition, when possible, five of the members must be voted on by the staff and two members can be appointed by administration. This ensures that the teachers have their representatives in addition to their elected union leader or teacher leader. The administrator selects two or three educators they believe can assist with the implementation of Shared Leadership.

Shared Leadership is also important to all support staff, counselors, social workers and psychologists within your building and not limited to just educators. Support staff must be represented when situations arise because they are the experts in their respective domains. For instance, if we are discussing implementing new testing procedures for special education, it is vital that we include the psychologist in any and all decisions to ensure we have support from them. The support of having everyone on the same page assists with creating and maintaining a culture that is conducive to student achievement. I have found it to be very impactful when the voting leadership team consists of just educators. However, garnering input from any and all school staff is vital to create a positive school culture.

Step 2: I began my very first leadership team meeting providing personal copies of the Diane Stanley book "*The Conversation Club.*" I provided about 20 minutes for the team to read this publication and outline or highlight key concepts in the book. We then discussed the importance of listening to one another, valuing each other's opinions and also providing ample wait time and ensuring no one was speaking over one another. The above became our norms for all leadership team meetings. We created the agenda for the next meeting and reviewed the school's vision statement. I also shared my personal vision statement which I committed to uphold.

Step 3: The average leadership team meetings consist of 60 minutes, bi-weekly. You can adjust this time as needed and as your educators are available. We have also implemented virtual meetings via Google Classroom or Blackboard which assist educators who have responsibilities at home. Recording meetings for those who are absent is beneficial, as well. The absentee member is then able to view the meeting in totality which will ensure he/she is up to date on the decisions that were made. I have always ensured there were funds in my school budget to pay educators for this valuable time and service. I find it imperative that you compensate your leadership team for the time they spend with you, improving the school as a whole.

Step 4: It is extremely important that these meetings do not become hijacked by non-instructional issues such as, how much to charge for pop in the lounge, or why the bake sale is on Thursday instead of Friday (I delegate these decisions to my teacher leader). To avoid said examples, it is imperative that you assign roles for each member of the leadership team so there is accountability at every meeting. You will definitely need a taskmaster who ensures that the meeting agenda always stays on target toward improved student achievement and school culture. To create a streamlined approach, all questions and ideas must be placed on the agenda, prior to the meeting, to ensure everyone is aware of what questions or topics will be discussed. This will ensure everyone has ample time to be prepared for the discussion. Normally, the person who was assigned as the secretary will take notes, record what decisions were agreed upon and create the next meeting agenda.

The next sub section I will discuss is a flow chart of the hierarchy of decision-making. I created this flow chart to be transparent with all educators and stakeholders. This upholds fidelity and ensures every idea has a fair chance of being discussed, and if agreed upon, implemented. I enlist my leadership team to ensure everyone's voice is heard. There is also a platform for sharing new ideas, academic concerns or items that can benefit student achievement or improve culture.

DECISION-MAKING
PROTOCOL GRAPHIC

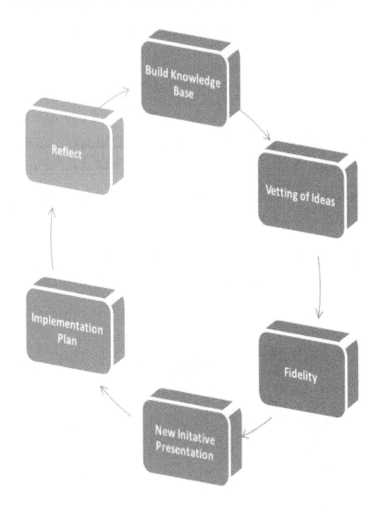

Decision-Making Protocols

Build Knowledge Base: In the beginning process of Shared Leadership Decision-Making, it is important that you research current trends vetted Evidence-Based practices for your school's demographics. As I have mentioned previously in other words, you are ensuring that you, as the Instructional Leader, have knowledge and resources to assist when educators bring questions or improvement ideas to the leadership team. While you certainly do not have to have answers to all of their questions, it is imperative, if you are to be viewed as an Instructional Leader, you have a strong current foundation in all areas of curriculum, data dissemination, assessment and current Evidence-Based teaching practices. Building a knowledge base is also where you have an opportunity to present some ideas for book studies, professional learning, new educational trends, and other best practices that have raised student achievement.

Vetting of Ideas: When new ideas are brought to you by the leadership team, it is important that you provide a fair and equitable discussion for each item. This includes ideas that may go against your vision for the school or the school's vision. As we work on questions or proposals, I always ask, "Does it relate to our school vision?" If the proposal or idea does not meet our vision, we normally will not entertain going further. The leadership team always provides feedback on the proposals at staff meetings or through my weekly staff notes. This ensures that all parties understand that their requests are presented and answered with fidelity. This is also a crucial step in building trust with your staff. As you move to the coaching role in Chapter Five, trust becomes a large part of educational willingness to implement Evidence-Based practices. The work you do with these processes will assist you in the forthcoming transformations.

Fidelity: After an item is brought to the leadership team and discussed, it is paramount that a vote by the leadership team is taken and recorded. Once a decision has been rendered, it can be documented to prevent any further issues. The notation of a vote ensures accuracy and also can be used should questions arise in the future. Once the leadership team decides they want to move forward with an idea, piece of curricula or other academic item, they should complete the 5 W's together.

New Initiative Presentation: Once the 5 W's are completed, you can begin on the implementation process with the entire staff. This consists of a presentation where you provide some key details of the new initiative while the teacher leader (elected union representative) discusses the reasoning and student achievement implication. When I present new initiatives with my teacher leader, I always open up with the background on the decisions and then allow him/her to discuss the instructional piece. When you get to the questions and answers portion, feel free to answer any questions, regardless of area, so it shows you are vested in the practice or additional practices. This ensures you will continue to show a unified front with your leadership team and entire staff.

Implementation Plan: If the new idea is a pilot amongst your leadership team, you share the trials and tribulations that the practice is going through. If it is a school-wide initiative, it is important that the leadership team and you create a professional learning plan, implementation timeline and expectations/success criteria. This will yield right into Chapter Five on coaching. Once an idea is implemented, you, as the Instructional Leader, become a coach to ensure the success criteria are met and that implementation is occurring under the same guise as how it was intended.

Reflect: Reflection and data study is one of the most vital steps to this hierarchy. This is to ensure what you are directing the educators to *keep doing or stop doing* (equivalent to exercise on pg. 43) is based on Evidence-Based practices and research. You also have to ensure the practice you and the leadership team chose has produced the results you had anticipated. This process of data dissemination will be covered exclusively in the next chapter. Fluency of data is the single biggest role for an Instructional Leader. You are the one responsible for disseminating the data as well as providing real time data to the staff. Your leadership team assists you with decisions regarding implementation of practices based on the data you collate. All of your decisions should be based upon the summative and formative data you have at your disposal. Once you have disseminated the data, you can then add the teacher formative and summative data. This is part of the Triangulation Model you will learn about in Chapter Four. This will ensure you continue to lead your school in the right direction toward increased student achievement.

As you look at using this Decision-Making Protocol, keep in mind there will be situations where educators bring ideas directly to you. This is fine, but your response should be that all decisions are made through the leadership team. Ensure you use the communication techniques we discussed in the last section to enable the staff member to feel valued and appreciated for bringing you an idea. I always ask educators and staff members to please email the idea to both the teacher leader and me so we are able to articulate their thoughts and discuss it at the next leadership team meeting. You will be inundated with new programs, ideas, etc. at various times. This Decision-Making Protocol will ensure all the ideas have their chance to be reviewed and discussed at the next leadership team meeting. I always found it much easier to pilot the select new ideas with the leadership team members, in lieu of asking the entire staff to implement something that has not been validated. Another reason I select a member of the leadership team to begin the implementation is it ensures me I have an excellent educator who will use this product or program with fidelity. The data we gather is as realistic for our demographics as possible. In other words, we are not using data directly from the company that may not contain the same socio-economic samples, race samples or other contributing factors. By having a leadership team member implement and collate data from his/her assessments, it shows a true depiction of what the results could be and are at your school. Regardless of how well you anticipate a program improving student achievement, it is always more impactful to use actual results that occurred at your building. This ensures fidelity in building-wide implementation. I would then empower the leadership team member who implemented or piloted the program to share his/her successes. This also allows for leadership capacity when full implementation occurs. You already have educators who have implemented this new initiative and they can help coach or show best practices for the adopted program.

Summary

In this chapter on Shared Leadership, I have provided a leadership team implementation process, shared decision-making process and strategies to delegate. While collaboration in itself is extremely beneficial, I also included my Decision-Making Protocol. The creation and implementation of a leadership team, along with you as the Instructional Leader focusing solely on academic issues, will take time to implement. Shared Leadership will transform your school truly becoming a holistic collaborative environment. Shared Leadership is one of the most instrumental practices that I implemented when I was hired as a principal. In retrospect, I was hired as principal at a dysfunctional school with an authoritarian approach. It took approximately two years to fully transform the entire staff into having trust in me and in this Shared Leadership process. The Shared Leadership process allowed the talents of all educators to be displayed and appreciated in a positive light.

The time and effort you spend creating a Shared Leadership environment will assist with the implementation of instructional strategies, solidifying instructional improvement of your school. This process has enabled me to implement strategies and practices more rapidly than trying to gain buy-in from each staff member.

I am available for consultation or virtual meetings. The purpose for writing this book, I believe, is to show how Instructional Leadership is the catalyst for school transformation.

Chapter 4

Data Warrior

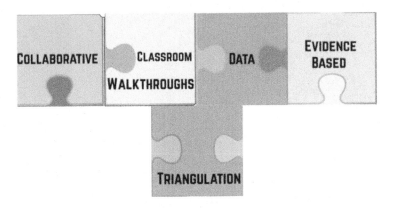

"If you can't explain it simply, you don't understand it well enough."

--Albert Einstein, Physicist

"A goal without a measurable outcome is like a sport competition without a score keeper."

--unknown

Triangulation of Data!!! Becoming a Data Warrior

No matter where you are in your educational journey, the one commonality we hear all the time is, "What does the data tell us?" We are provided almost too much data in today's schools, making the dissemination and vetting process of data even more important than collecting it. As I tell mentees and educators, not all data is good data. Data that is not norm-referenced or based on specific standards is less impactful.

There is no replacement for effective educators using impactful Evidence-Based practices. **Evidence-Based practices unequivocally are the only processes that will lead to immense student achievement.** I will further explain in Chapter Six some of the strategies with the highest impact that have been vetted by myself and through meta-analysis.

In this chapter, I will walk you through how we use data, how I coach data usage and what to look for in improving school-level data. I have been known to be a "data nerd" in my district. I constantly have data on the school walls, on my desk and even carry my impact sheets with me when in the hall working with students. Here are a few examples of data that I deem important:

- State Assessments
- Quarterly Assessments (NWEA, STAR, I-Ready, Terra Nova, Semester or Quarterly exams, etc.)
- Most important formative assessments provided by educators (pre-test, post-tests)
- High Schools should begin to disseminate eighth-grade data and not wait for ninth-grade assessments. As we know from research, ninth grade is the most critical grade in high school. I have found that if

students start out performing poorly academically in ninth grade, their future success is hindered.

- If you are a mastery-based school or use mastery practices from our other publication "*Mastery-Based Mathematics*," using the mastery checks and assessments are great tools for collecting data.

In this section, you will be presented with my Triangulation of Data Chart. This data chart consists of the following data sources:

- Teacher Level Summative and Formative Assessments
- State and Norm-Referenced Assessments
- Classroom Observation (walk-throughs) of Teaching Practices

This data chart will show which sources of data should be used to form a complete picture of student achievement. Data charts are paramount when using data to make decisions. It is equally important to use multiple pieces of data to ensure you have the complete picture of the data being measured. Each section of the Triangulation Data Chart is of equal importance. Ensure when reviewing data, one is not considered more important than the others. They are all necessary to insure you have the complete portfolio to determine student achievement. We want all decisions to be based on at least three data points to ensure fidelity. This will present a complete picture of school, educator and student achievement.

Triangulation of Data Chart

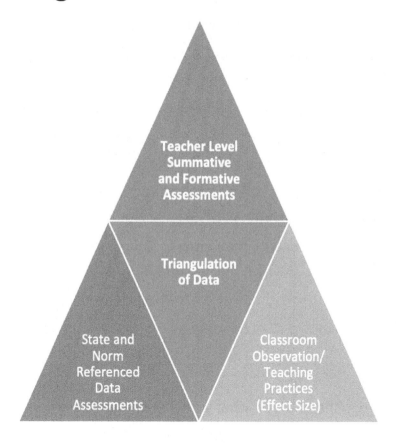

It is vital that everyone is looking at the same data. You cannot have data conversations without having consistent summative assessments.

How to Implement a Data Mindset in Your School

As an Instructional Leader or aspiring Instructional Leader, data dissemination is vital to your success. Let's delve into one specific piece of data that affects most schools' state ratings. State report cards are visible to all stakeholders within the school district community and the state. Due to numerous governmental initiatives like *No Child Left Behind* and *Every Student Succeeds Act* (ESSA), data reporting at the state level is mandatory. In data workshops where I facilitate leaders, I start with the following seven processes. This should be completed prior to the leader rolling the information out to his/her staff. Do not hand out state data to your staff and expect a clear understanding of the information. Data conversations are one of the vital components to school success and educator improvement. This data should be disseminated by the Instructional Leader prior to roll out.

First: Breakdown all of the data by grade level and teacher level.

Second: Check to see what your state considers a full year student (i.e., If a student enters in February, they normally do not count toward the passing percentage of the grade level). Remove all the students who do not fit this criterion as this will cause the data to skew. This also will inhibit data conversations as the focus will be on incomplete parts of the data not on student achievement. This will most likely be the first thing the educators point out as the student or students were not there all year. It can also adversely skew the data for high transient or large schools.

This exercise will also ensure your school's as well as your district's EMIS or attendance reconciliation system is correct. I have worked with numerous districts whose attendance data is incorrect and it causes scores to be adversely affected. Do not think of this as a district role. You must ensure the data that goes into the attendance system is correct and student's removal is completed correctly and timely.

Third: Once you have the data separated by classroom educator, it is time to review the other pieces of data. For instance, if you use a quarterly assessment that predicts how the students will finish on the spring test, then compare that data to see if it was correct. In other words, this will assist you with validating the quarterly assessments as a valid predictor of student achievement on state assessments. I am critical of some quarterly assessments that predict 70% of students will pass but then 50% actually pass. There should be no more than about a 7-10% variance. Quarterly assessment products are available and listed in my data sources above. The assessment products I notated earlier have vetted research that is norm-referenced. As a leader, this ensures that the assessments you provide for your learners are consistent and reliable to predict student outcomes. You are looking for what is called a linkage report or study. For example, if I have an educator who improved more than 7-10% over last year's data, I am going to look and see if he/she implemented a new practice.

Fourth: This is where data collation can get a bit "messy" when not using computer growth metrics. The reason I like to look at percentage passing is because that's what the state reports to the public. The community may like to see that the school grew 15%, but that's a hard sell when you only have 25% passing the assessment.

Growth and Proficiency in my eyes are totally different. Growth is important and can be the catalyst for proficiency. Using growth, however, as a metric for saying a school is successful, in my opinion, is not valid. This is controversial as most people are happy if their students show growth. Leaders will focus on the growth and we know from educational research all students grow just by coming to school. If you truly are focused on growth, look at which students or grade levels had more than one year's growth in one year's time. That will ensure that the data you have is showing true impact by each educator.

Fifth: Should we compare last year's learners to this year's learners? I have observed numerous leaders compare last year's fourth-grade scores to this year's fourth-grade scores and form their opinions of educators based on that data. That is mathematically incorrect. When using data over multiple years, you should be studying cohorts of students, not looking at specific grade levels. Here is a basic spread sheet set up to give you a visual. For this, I will use a scaled score which is very common for all state and quarterly assessments to use as a metric. These scores can also be converted to grade-level proficiency metrics by state.

Student	2018 score (3rd Grade)	2019 score (4th Grade)	Result
Joe Unknown	624 (Not Pass)	701 (Pass)	Large Growth
Charlie Brown	724 (Pass)	744 (Pass Accelerated)	Large Growth
Lucy	724 (Pass)	724 (Pass)	Growth

So, as I am working with educators and presenting this data information, we glean numerous things just from this information. The first thing noticed is that the educator showed more than one year's growth in one year's time with Joe and

Charlie. He/She also showed growth with Lucy. Lucy grew at the same rate as in the previous year. I would deem this educator a top educator. I would be looking to see what instructional strategies he/she is using and to engage him/her in conversations around instructional practices.

Sixth: Educators will want to know how they measured compared to last year. It is important that you explain the above information to them and state that we are studying cohorts of students. Comparing cohorts ensure that the variables are consistent or as some educators state, "Comparing apples to apples." However, I ensure the focus is on the students who scored *proficient* or *passing*. These are small wins every time they occur and can lead to large gains in a school's performance the more times they occur. When it's time to look at granular data, we look at specific standards from previous years as well as current data to see where assistance is needed. By looking at granular data, you should be able to find a few standards where educators excelled as well as areas for refinement. I will provide another chart to help explain.

Student	4. NBTA.1 (Place Value)	4.MD.A.1 (Measurement Conversions)	Result
Joe Unknown	Strong/Pass	Weak/ Fail 0 out of 3	Did not cover
Charlie Brown	Strong/ Pass	Barely Pass 2 out of 3	Self-Paced
Lucy	Strong/Pass	Weak/ Fail 1 out of 3	Did not cover

So, once again, I collated the above data and when I had a data meeting with educators, we brainstormed on what occurred at each standard. We began with some questions such as:

- Where did each standard fall in the scope of the year?
- Did we not have time to teach a standard(s)?
- Can we use a computer program to assist with remediation and acceleration for a standard?
- Is pacing too fast for some topics and too slow for others?

These are the types of data questions that the Instructional Leaders can use to advocate for Evidence-Based.

practices. Instructional Leaders can also congratulate educators on their amazing instruction.

"Proficiency opens doors that growth cannot."
-Jack Hunter

Seventh: Once this data information has been disseminated and I have met with every educator, it is time to share this information for planning purposes with the leadership team. This assessment data is strictly one piece of the triangulation. The collection of data on standards can be used to look at whole-year summative data for the leadership team to solicit professional learning based upon what areas the school has underperformed. Also, look for professional learning where educators might have some room for immense growth.

Leadership Team Data Meetings

Step One: When presenting data to the leadership team, separate each report by content areas and grade levels. For instance, if we have four math teachers at grade four, is there a correlation in a specific area such as geometry or inferencing where all students struggle? If so, this is where the leadership team needs to spring into action. Within the leadership team model, we begin to look at the needs for professional learning in the area where learners struggle. We also review the data to see if an educator on staff has shown exemplary data where we could empower him/her to share best practices with other staff members.

This is also time for the Instructional Leader to research current publications and curricula strategies that may provide insight into the areas where the school struggled. For instance, if I noticed that the students struggled with citing text evidence, I would look for graphic organizers, such as "RACES", to help students understand what evidence is and how you can properly cite it in writing.

As I dissected the data for the leadership team, I provided the bottom two standards or strands and the top two standards or strands. We then began to look at curriculum maps which are akin to some district's pacing guides. We divided the standards among the leadership team based on content areas and prepared to share this information with the entire staff. In lieu of just handing out data and saying it was good or bad, the goal is to share two pieces of evidence that show growth and two pieces of evidence that show room for improvement. It is important to not "spoil" the findings of individual educators looking at the data; however, you can overwhelm nondate-minded people with just handing them pages of data. Data Analysis needs to be taught as well, which is part of the role as the Instructional Leader. We wanted to share this information on standards or strands so educators could evaluate for themselves if there was a gap in the curriculum, or if they simply did not have enough time to cover the topic. The exercise also provided information to the previous year's educator. This way, they can evaluate individual student's strengths and weaknesses and decide when they needed to go deeper by standard. This practice assisted educators with being adaptive to the needs of the learners who were assigned to them. We also looked to see if the content coverage occurred after the summative testing.

I hear quite frequently that school is not all about the tests. My response is always the same, "High test scores open up doors for our students." We don't make the rules, but we do have to play by them. Instead of getting on that bandwagon, embrace the rules and work within the confines to help your educators and students succeed.

Step Two: Everything must go through your Decision-Making Protocol (Chapter Three). This is specifically why it is important for you to collate and disseminate the data so you have a thorough understanding of each grade level's strengths and weaknesses. This ensures when professional learning or curricula is selected, it meets the area deemed deficient.

Step Three: Once you have provided the disseminated data to your staff and your leadership team discusses the school and district curriculum, data, and teacher-level data (this will take more than one meeting), you can then begin to make decisions to assist with student growth.

1. Adopt specific curricula add-ons to address the shortfalls. No curriculum is 100% perfect, so instead of buying new curricula, just supplement by the standards that are deficient.

2. Look for professional learning for the necessary standards to remediate the area where students or educators struggled.

3. Begin to look for specific strategies by individual teachers to help improve the non-proficient areas. This is how we eventually selected Reciprocal Teaching (discussed in detail in Chapter Six) as it hits every single content area and has a high effect size. It also was easily implemented.

4. As a leader, have quarterly data meetings with your learners. This may seem arduous with a school of over 800 kids or more, however, it is very beneficial. This can occur at the teacher level but it also must occur at the administrative level. I always advise my mentees that if they have less than 400 students in grades 3-8, you can easily handle this over a 9-week period. This equates to roughly 45 students a week or nine per day. Each conversation should take 2-3 minutes at the

most. You are going to review the latest summative data and ask the students to predict where they believe their strengths and weaknesses lie. You then have each student write two learning targets or goals he/she will strive to improve. Have each one sign it and keep it in a binder by classroom (This can be housed in the teacher's classroom should you choose).

I always keep this data in my office in case I need to conference with a student or parent. I have the most current data available to ensure when I converse with stakeholders, the information is relevant. It is much easier to converse with parents when you have non-subjective norm-referenced data instead of having them discuss a teacher's assignment. I never discount my educators' assignments, however, when parents question the validity of a grade, I always check to see if the students' norm-referenced data match what the parent is insinuating. As always, there are outliers and each student must be evaluated on a student-by-student basis.

Growth = Proficiency

As stated before, I believe that proficiency is the ultimate metric for student achievement. However, there are some exceptions when growth does supersede proficiency. I would be a miss to think that every student with a disability can pass his or her state test. Keeping true to the vision of our school, we believe that talent can be hidden anywhere. We have numerous students with disabilities who excel in areas such as computer science and project-based learning. This is why the study of cohorts of students is so vital to paint a true picture of the educator and the child. One thing I can tell you is that a student's label should not drive his/her instruction. For example, if a student has a behavior goal, the goal should not determine the student's instructional level capability. Having all educators understand that a behavior goal does not determine the level of instruction that the student deserves or is capable of will certainly raise student achievement. As we discussed in Chapter One, a fixed mindset will yield minimal growth. But a growth mindset, for instance, believing that student's behavior goal is not indicative of their intellect level, will assist students and the school community with improving the students' performance. We will learn about changing one life with a starfish story in Chapter Five. Student's assessment should drive their instruction. Believing in the growth mindset of all learners truly assisted us in exceeding all preconceived expectations of special education learners. I stand firmly and believe any student can exceed one year's growth in one year's time if the educator uses the correct strategies and the school is focused on its vision.

Yes, IEP plans assist in providing a map for the student's learning, but the key is to scaffold grade-level content for the student to be successful. Through data collection, there are numerous times where I notice that a special education student is above average on certain standards or topics. With current data, educators are able to accelerate past these standards and spend more time remediating the areas where the data shows the student is deficient or struggling. By understanding and providing the correct interventions, scaffolding and support, students with disabilities can be more successful when they are mainstreamed into the general education classroom. One of Hattie's most impactful studies was done with students with disabilities being provided high impact instructional strategies, including direct instruction and feedback to students.

Inequity Sparks the Action

I feel the need to provide some information on the process I created one summer while immersed in Hattie's, Marzano's and Viviane Robinson's research. After struggling to move the academic needle for all learners in math, I knew I had to think outside the box. Noticing a large inequity between where our learners scored on state mathematics assessments, it became apparent that they lacked the background knowledge and rigorous instruction to make up the more than one year grade level they were behind. This inequity required a new approach to teaching mathematics that would assist our educators and learners with producing more than one year's growth in one years' time. Ideas I gleaned from the above researches led me to create the framework known as Mastery-Based Mathematics. Mastery-Based Mathematics uses formative and summative assessments to determine their current academic areas of strengths and weaknesses and allows the learner to progress at their own pace. This framework allows intervention, acceleration and remediation to occur simultaneously based on where their strengths and weaknesses lie. I created Mastery-Based Learning in Mathematics. I approached a leadership team member to pilot this new evidence and research-based strategy. It was so successful, this educator and I were asked to publish a book. We have presented on Mastery-Based Mathematics numerous times at conferences. It truly changed the trajectory of math instruction in our school and later went on to change the entire culture in all content areas. There is far too much information on Mastery-Based Mathematics to summarize from the previous book, but sharing graphics will help you derive the topics.

Here is a flowchart of the progressions we use through our Mastery Process. The Mastery strategy will be explained in Chapter Six.

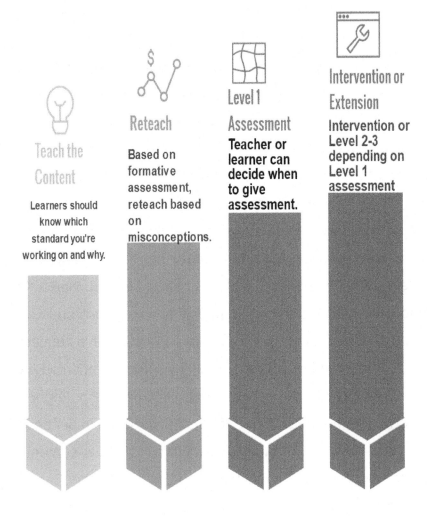

Teach the Content

Learners should know which standard you're working on and why.

Reteach

Based on formative assessment, reteach based on misconceptions.

Level 1 Assessment

Teacher or learner can decide when to give assessment.

Intervention or Extension

Intervention or Level 2-3 depending on Level 1 assessment

After each step, formative assessments should be taking place. After Level 1 is passed, new content can be instructed

We judge our barometer of excellence purely on normative data from at least three sources of information such as NWEA, STAR, formative assessments and state assessments. As you can see, it is not until you get to step 4 where new content begins.

Walk-Throughs (Learning Walks)

A walk-through is defined as short, focused, and informal observations of student's involvement in the lesson, instructional strategies utilized by the educator and climate of the classroom. As a school leader, you should be able to answer the following questions after completing a walk-through:

- Are students learning?
- Do some educators deserve special positive reinforcement?
- Are educators on track with the curriculum?
- Do some educators need redirection or emergency support for behavior?

During daily walk-throughs throughout my building, I take numerous mental notes. I jot down positive reinforcement thoughts to share with the classroom educator. These comments are always academically informative for the educators and me. Examples of the comments I notate are as follows:

- ➢ Excellent high quality question on_____.
- ➢ Excellent wait time of 5 seconds or more for student response.
- ➢ Objective is aligned to the benchmark standard.
- ➢ Very nice job of using more than one instructional strategy to explain_____.
- ➢ Differentiation was noticed; you may also want to try different instructional groupings. I witnessed a few learners who were off task.
- ➢ Fantastic job of the "You DO" portion of the lesson being differentiated. Kudos for having levels of work and assessment.
- ➢ It was empowering to see you managing the classroom by rotating to each learner and managing by proximity.
- ➢ Amazing! All of your learners were engaged!

For instance, conducting walk-throughs and seeing a new practice being attempted, provide a thumbs up to the educator. Immediately write a handwritten note thanking and praising the educator for trying something new. Leaders should use this time while conducting walk-throughs to point out other positive observations in the classroom. This is not analytical data and can be subjective; however, summative and formative data normally support the classroom walkthrough observations.

I spend about 60% of my time in classrooms during the day observing practices, student behavior and student engagement levels. Walk-throughs provide specific data and provides me the pulse of the learning environment. Data is not all analytical and the "sense" you glean from walk-throughs and visits with students will confirm what the data is showing you on state-wide assessments.

Walk-throughs are a continuous cycle that should be used for school improvement by focusing on all the effects of instruction. It is also important to speak with students as you are conducting walk-throughs. This should be done quietly to not shift the focus away from the learning. Some of the questions I ask are:

- ✓ How does the educator contribute to your learning?
- ✓ What is your grade in this subject and why? (Older kids)
- ✓ How can you use what you are learning when you are not in school?
- ✓ Does the school and teacher offer you an opportunity for growth?

These questions are just a few that assist me with garnering a more complete picture of the learning that is taking place in the classrooms.

While working with mentees and tracking their time usage, I have found that they spend their time on the following:

1. Office   65%
2. Out of school meetings   12%
3. Hallways   16%
4. Classrooms   7%

My simple message is that the times should be switched between the fourth and first. At least 65% of your time should be spent in classrooms. I empower all leaders to conduct at least 10 walk-throughs per day for no more than three to five minutes each. You must keep track of when and how frequently you visit each classroom to ensure equity and that educators feel they are non-evaluative. As a leader, I visit all of my classrooms at least twice per day. I also will become involved in the learning, but this is something that must be worked up to. An example is chiming in and helping to explain content or working one-to-one with a learners who is struggling. The educators and learners must begin to see you as an Instructional Leader.

I will provide additional ideas on how to use coaching to improve classroom walk-throughs. A few key points to remember when implementing walk-throughs:

1. They are not evaluative and the purpose is to improve student learning.

2. Make them positive by providing at least two positive notes.
3. Be consistent and ensure no one has walk-throughs completed more than anyone else.
4. Summarize findings from walk-throughs for the leadership team about instruction only.

Summary

Looking back on areas of growth from this chapter, you should be able to:
1. Disseminate Data
2. Delegate more
3. Spend more time in classrooms
4. Refer to Triangulation Chart when making decisions

Creating and maintaining a data dashboard was one of the first pieces of the data puzzle. I started by placing current trend data on a whiteboard in the hallway. This showed which classroom improved the most on quarterly assessments. Each class made a prediction on what their passage rate would be on the state exams. This visual reminder allowed everyone to understand that we were academically focused. It is the responsibility of the principal to instruct staff members and stakeholders on the data that is most relevant.

Refrain from making predictions that are not backed up by current data. These exercises of disseminating data occur every quarter when new summative data is available. This ensures adjustments can be made by the Instructional Leader and the leadership team to assist with student achievement.

Numerous educational computer programs are available and all promise the same outcomes of increased student learning. Through research, we have found that computer programs have a very small effect size on student achievement. John Hattie, through his meta-analysis, has found the effect size of the average computer program instruction to have a .37 effect size. We know that anything below a .4 effect size is not ideal. There is some value to educational computer programs when used as reinforcement to excellent instruction. As a leader, it is paramount that you do not look for these types of programs to be a silver bullet.

New curriculum implementation has to be watched and managed closely as educators need proper professional learning on the implementation of new curricula. Once again, please do not just buy a product or educational program that claims to solve a problem. **"Educators are the catalyst for change and with strong Instructional Leadership; together you can find the key pieces that yield more than one year's growth in one year's time."**

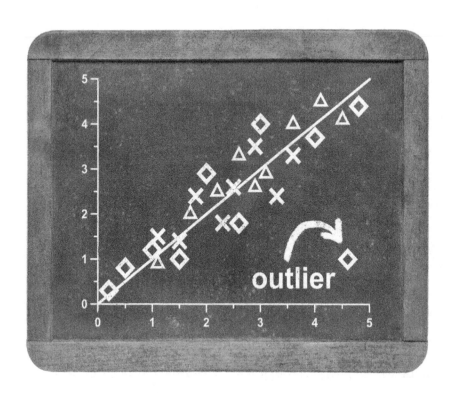

Chapter 5

Coaching

"Coaching is unlocking people's potential to maximize their own performance. It is helping them to learn rather than teaching them."
--John Whitmore

So, when I think about what skills make an effective coach, I think of Captain D. Michael Abrashoff, the former commander of the USS Benfold. The first step Abrashoff used was building trust. This is just as relevant for Instructional Leadership, as well. He would ask himself the following questions when he did not get the results he wanted after a meeting or event:

1. Did I clearly articulate the goals?
2. Did I give people enough time and resources to accomplish the task?
3. Did I give them enough training?

He discovered when visions or events failed, he was 90% of the reason why the vision failed. Think about the impact this self-reflection had on his entire Navy command. He was commanding a warship and was humble enough to realize and reflect.

I wish to define what coaching is and what coaching is not, so we can be clear of the expectations when it comes to you as an Instructional Leader.

Coaching is:

1. Ensuring the expectations are realistic and follow the SMART Goal guidelines.
2. Providing feedback to the person you are coaching.
3. Providing continual support, not a one and done approach or occasional check-in check-out.
4. Enabling people being coached to have some control on what specifics they are being coached.
5. Relating all coaching to the specific job duties of the person being coached.
6. Providing motivation and emotional support in an environment that promotes growth through mistake-based learning.

Coaching is not:

1. Training: The work you are doing is specific to each individual you are coaching. While you may be coaching on a specific piece of curriculum, it will look different for every educator you are coaching. Some educators may need a more granular style of coaching, while others may need assistance with working in a risk-free environment.

2. Supervision: While coaching, you are not looking for things that the educator did or does incorrectly. You should focus on the common goal that was created between you and the educator, based solely on data or evidence and agreed upon prior to starting the coaching.

3. Water Cooler: This is not a time for learning about everything that is happening in the life of the person you are coaching. Allow no more than 90 seconds for the person to share a story and then relate the conversation back to the topic at hand. This is vital or you can be consumed with water cooler talk and little will be accomplished on coaching and improving educational practice.

The lesson to learn here is if the person we are coaching or helping is failing; we are partly to blame for the failure. This goes for all instruction and activities that happen in our buildings. It is impossible for you as an Instructional Leader to watch every lesson, student interaction, parent interaction, etc. Coaching should point out academic items educators have done well, mastered or what they may need support on. It should not be a time to just focus on what did not work. Most importantly, as Instructional Leaders you must be willing to do all the tasks we ask our staff to complete.

The first rule of being a good coach is to establish trust. When you show competence and vulnerability, you begin to build trust. Educators want you to have all the answers but also want to be able to problem solve with you. It is alright to not have a solution; sometimes the problem solving process creates far more trust than just providing a solution to the problem.

While coaching and conducting walk-throughs, I may notice an educator doing something that is outside the norm. This is when I like to complete what is called a *Positive Referral*. Write a quick note and place it in the box for afternoon announcements. Read the positive note on the afternoon announcements. The students in their classrooms always cheer. Attempt to complete at least three positive referrals a week. This goes a long way in celebrating staff success. Place a small candy bar in their mailbox with the positive referral. I notice these positive notes hanging next to the teacher's desk. It shows how impactful positive energy and acknowledgment is for your staff. Coaching without trust will not yield change! Coaching with trust will change the future of your students, educators and community.

As you are working on building trust, which is the foundation of coaching, here are a few lessons and non-negotiable communication skills that must happen to build trust:

- Be an active listener.
- Do not interrupt!
- Do not make body movements (Remember the communication protocols in Chapter Two)!

It is ok to take notes and ask for clarifying points to understand their statements. If the person you are coaching asks for something and you agree, make sure it is done immediately.

I use the above communication skills at staff meetings or anytime I interact with educators. I started small and knew I could empower and coach for this mindset to be everlasting. The above communication strategies are just as important with new educators or guest educators who are in your building. You only have a few seconds to make a first impression. Your active listening skills can speed up trust, with new educators or staff members in your building. I think of the importance of communication skills when meeting someone for the first time. The person's opinion of you will be formed very quickly.

I have worked extremely hard on building content strengths in all curriculum areas other than math (I am a former math educator). When I have a firm handle on academic data and the background knowledge on curriculum to consult educators, I know I can begin the coaching process. I completed the majority of this content capacity, building over the summer of my first year as a principal. When I came back to school the following year, I used this story to motivate staff to make small changes and also to look at each student as their own challenge:

Once upon a time, there was an old man who used to go to the ocean to do his writing. He had a habit of walking on the beach every morning before he began his work. Early one morning, he was walking along the shore after a big storm had passed and found the vast beach littered with starfish as far as the eye could see, stretching in both directions.

Off in the distance, the old man noticed a small boy approaching. As the boy walked, he paused every so often and as he grew closer, the man could see that he was occasionally bending down to pick up an object and throw it into the sea. The boy came closer still and the man called out, "Good morning! May I ask what it is that you are doing?"

The young boy paused, looked up, and replied, "Throwing starfish into the ocean. The tide has washed them up onto the beach and they can't return to the sea by themselves," the youth replied. "When the sun gets high, they will die, unless I throw them back into the water."

The old man replied, "But there must be tens of thousands of starfish on this beach. I'm afraid you won't really be able to make much of a difference."

The boy bent down, picked up yet another starfish and threw it as far as he could into the ocean. Then he turned, smiled and said, "It made a difference to that one!"

I used the adage that we can make a difference in the lives of children. If we change one child's life, it is worth all of our efforts, trials and tribulations. I purchased every staff member a starfish pin (as pictured below). I asked staff to wear the pin or keep it somewhere to remind them how special they are and how they can change one student's life or academic experience.

I also purchased mini-starfish and would tape them on a handwritten note when I noticed educators trying a new strategy or doing something that exceeded the norm. I wanted to show them I was aware of how they were changing their practice. This continued to create a culture of growth and also allowed me the opportunity to coach. Sometimes the simplest things are the most impactful!

This quote from NBA coach Phil Jackson, who coached Michael Jordan and Kobe Bryant stated: *"I think the most important thing about coaching is that you have to have a sense of confidence about what you're doing. You have to be a salesman and you have to get your players, particularly your leaders, to believe in what you're trying to accomplish on the basketball floor."*

The communication changes you made in Chapter Two will pay dividends now as you try to build community and trust with your staff. Using a simple story and a pin created a sense of momentum that engaged even some of the reluctant educators. I used these starfish and notes to positively reinforce the educators. Staff was able to perceive me as a positive adage to our vision. They began to see me as a coach who was trying to uncover their hidden talents!

I have given a few examples of what coaching is and how I began to build a sense of trust with staff. I also have shown you a unique way that assists the staff with focusing on changing one student's life. Next, I will delve into what needs to take place when you are asked to model a lesson for example, or you notice that an educator is struggling with a content area or standard.

I was conducting a walk-through in a fifth-grade math class and the educator was struggling with teaching fractions. He/She was puzzled and it was obvious the students were frustrated. Instead of jumping in and stealing his/her "power", I purchased a very good book on fractions and provided it to him/her as a resource. I then asked the educator if I could read the book when he/she was finished. This way I could provide support. We ended up having a book talk about the fraction publication. We developed a symbiotic relationship and to this day we can share feedback with each other. Something as simple as purchasing a book and asking if I could read it when he/she was finished opened up a conversation that is still built on trust and coaching to this day.

Educators Who Are Slow to Embrace Coaching!

I have a few educators that were reluctant to welcome coaching. For this group of educators, I conducted a book study on Robert Marzano's, "*Reflective Educator.*" This book is single handily the best tool you could ever purchase to help reluctant educators self-reflect. Of course it is a great tool for all educators which is why all educators were invited to participate. This book study occurred after school and some meetings before school at a coffee shop. All educators who attended were compensated and also received contact hours.

We began with the self-reflection tool. We launched into discussing how Marzano's work and Hattie's work on self-reflection lead to pedagogical changes in the educators who implemented them. I was amazed at how many educators presented items they currently were instructing or thought about implementing concerning assessment. This provided a great platform for collaboration while also building trust. These were conversations outside the scope of evaluation. Simply put, I made a statement that we are just a group of educators who are using Evidence-Based Strategies from research to further improve our practice and drive change in our students' learning. Marzano's self-reflection tool builds trust between the coach and the coachee. It also creates self-reflection and awareness of the teachers' own strengths and weaknesses.

Top Educators Who Are Used to Working in Silos!

I have some amazing educators who are highly effective based on the Triangulation Model of Data Collection. They produce quality results and are amiable, collaborative partners. Top educators continue to produce at a high level and strive for more than one year's growth in one year's time. I needed these educators to become leaders in their field and in the building.

As I was conducting learning walks, I noticed educators were attempting to implement these practices (Evidence-Based practices discussed in Chapter Six). I knew I had to begin the coaching process to ensure everyone had the opportunity to implement these Evidence-Based Practices (discussed in Chapter Six) and the support they needed. I empowered educators who were implementing these practices currently and producing high results to assist me in modeling the practices. In addition, I asked them to assist me in demonstrating the evidence they had on student achievement. Even though the data contained a small sample size, it is important to celebrate any positive moments (small wins) you have when implementing new practices. This became a part of our regular meeting itinerary and we called it a "best practice share out." I believe all educators learn best when they share amongst their peers. We would discuss what Evidence-Based Practices he/she was implementing and the results. I would ask these leading educators to try new practices. They always embraced new ideas as they wanted to be challenged as well. The talent was already there; it was just covered up by not sharing their magnificent work. By uncovering the talents of the existing staff, educator efficiency began to improve and staff began to welcome new perspectives. Being able to go into a teacher's room and encourage them to try a new practice requires the administration to have current, relevant and appropriate background knowledge on the topic. It also requires trust from the educator.

Data Conversations and Coaching Are Symbiotic

When you begin to work with educators and student-level data, it is imperative that you use this time to "coach" the educator. It can be overwhelming for an educator who has instructed all year to receive less than stellar student scores. The importance for the Instructional Leader is to assist the educator with implementing practices that will yield higher student achievement. While sharing data with educators, I strongly encourage you to find three positive pieces of data in a data set for every one piece of data that you want to investigate. Look for positive outliers to ensure the conversation stays positive and trust continues to build. The language you use to communicate with the person being coached should be of an empowering nature. In the next section, you will be provided with a data sharing activity which will assist you in having data conversations.

Building the Trust While Sharing Data

Activity: *Build a community of educators who value data as a performance-metric and self-evaluation tool.*
Using the ideas I shared earlier in this chapter, you have laid a foundation of trust which opens the door to coaching and decision-making based on data. It is now time to make the foundation even stronger and begin to tell a story with the data. This data sharing activity should be completed approximately one month after staff has created their vision.

First: Collate data from the most recent state and quarterly assessments. For instance, if you are conducting this activity in October, you will use last year's summative data and this year's first quarterly assessment (do not hold this activity until 1st quarter's quarterly assessments are completed). This is important as you can review the growth that was lost due to the summer slide or students who moved out of your school district. This is paramount as you ask your educators and leadership team to forecast growth, including those students who are new to the building. If you do have new students, ensure you get their test scores from the state or previous school. Your educators need this data and you should have an administrative person track it down for you.

Second: Provide summative data to the previous year's teachers so they can reflect on their practice. This information will also assist educators later as they work in vertical PLCs (Chapter Six). Educators will need time to granularly discuss the strengths and weaknesses of each learner (Chapter Six). ***Just to clarify, in the first step, you are providing current data (most recent state assessment data is deemed current). In step two, you are providing the previous year's and current state data to the previous year's educator.*

Example: Teacher A teaches 7th grade. He/She receives data on the current eighth graders to reflect and also receives data on the incoming seventh graders to plan.

Third: Provide ample time of at least 30 minutes for educators to digest and ask questions on the data. This can include staff meetings, PLCs or district mandated time. There will be questions that arise and being present ensures the educators feel comfortable with the data. It is important that you do not just hand out the data and retreat to your office. This is a school-wide activity and one in which you, as the Instructional Leader, must be present physically and mentally. I never recommend providing more than quarterly assessment data and state data at this time for planning meetings. Providing too many pieces of data to review at one time is overwhelming when you are looking at multiple grade levels. The granular focus on triangulation will occur during teacher meeting time or PLCs (Chapter Six). All of these practices can be utilized Kindergarten through twelfth grade and may require slight adaptation.

Fourth: During data sharing, always ask educators if there was one student who was the "*outlier*". Did they notice, just by this quick overview, one student who exceeded the results from the previous year? Did they grow more than one year in one year's time? When the educator finds the *outlier*, I review the data and then write the name down. At the end of the meeting, I share the name of one of the students and celebrate the success of the educator. I will normally show the student's previous scaled score and compare it to the most recent improvement. I will have the educator stand up and be recognized by the staff for assisting with the student improvement. This is huge as it causes educators to look at the *outlier*, which is what we should be studying in data.

I remember one statement I heard a long time ago at a presentation: "4 out of 5 dentists recommend _____toothpaste." I wonder what the other one knows that the other four do not? Change occurs when we study the *outlier* and delve into what caused the extraordinary change.

Fifth: Each week on my school happenings news bulletin, I provide a snippet of a student who out-produced a grade-level standard.

Sixth: Continue the data conversations while you visit classrooms, meetings and events. Data discussions can produce terrific insights that will truly uncover hidden talents around you! All of this is accomplished by building trust with educators and using data to drive instruction.

Building Coaching Capacity

When beginning to coach educators who might be struggling or have identified areas where they need assistance to show growth, here are a few things to remember. **The staff needs to be a part of creating the objectives for their improvement.** You cannot assume the person who needs coaching wants coaching or believes you are the best candidate to provide it. They need examples from other stakeholders on how working with you has yielded success. This is why it is so important to start small. Your educators who you consider your top educators are a great place to start. Start coaching your top educators. You will notice that other educators, who are high producers, and growth oriented, will strive for your educational and curriculum support. You will begin to transform your staff from the inside out. Adults must be in control of what they learn.

Remember, as you read the above information, being an effective coach relies on data and not just the Instructional Leader's opinion.

Coaching Struggling Educators

My leadership team and I disseminated reading data over a two-year period and noticed a seasoned, veteran educator struggling with improving his/her students' reading scores. He/She attended numerous professional learning sessions, had over 25 hours of teacher-based team meetings, as well as district mandated learning. He/She had impeccable classroom management where the kids were compliantly bored.

The leadership team and I decided to meet with the educator. We informed him/her the impact his/her teaching strategies were having on student achievement. To show a unified front, the teacher union representative also accompanied to ensure the communication was properly delivered. I always request to have another adult, normally the union representative, present when I have a discussion based on performance.

He/She was given one goal to improve upon that year. As I suspected, about mid-way through the conversation, he/she began to cry. It is hard to watch someone you care about cry. However, it is not fair to the children you serve to allow ineffective practices to taint their potential. After listening empathetically, we suggested a goal of working with a mentor in the building and focusing on one strategy for reading. We provided all the resources for him/her to start guided reading in small groups to help him/her differentiate the learning. In the past, the educator would have all the students read in round robin, which we all know is one of the least effective practices. She/He eventually realized how effective Guided Reading was and how much the learners enjoyed working in groups.

As a leadership team, we noticed how his/her demeanor improved and she/he even seemed happier when interacting with his/her students. When this instructor gave the quarterly assessments, he/she showed student growth that exceeded 15%, which was higher than at the same time last year. This was a cause for celebration. The teacher leader (Union Representative) delivered two large chocolate bars and a congratulations to the teacher on the changes he/she made for herself/himself and the children he/she serves.

In some non-productive environments, these types of conversations would consist of managers, for example, telling their employees to improve as their data is underwhelming. Or possibly, the administrator would just complain about the educator and agree to do nothing as the conversation might not work or hurt personal feelings.

All conversations need to be had. This does not mean they will be easy, but they are necessary. Ron Clark states in his book, *Move the Bus*, "You can spend your time at school however you choose, but you only get to spend it once." Such a powerful statement to make when we only have our learners 180 days or less per year. This is your time, as an Instructional Leader, to ensure every student that comes in your building gets to learn from an educator who works to the successful development of the children. Your work is never done. **Coaches never stop coaching. Leaders never stop leading. It starts and ends with you!**

As an avid sports fan, I like to use sports analytics and scenarios to help people understand what we as humans are capable of achieving. Did you know that if you were playing a basketball game, it is better to be down by 1 point at halftime than up by 2 points? It is an analytical fact. The behavior science behind it proves that humans want to overcome the scenarios in front of them. Coaches are able to use positive analogies to inspire their team to make one fewer mistake so their team could be in the lead.

I liken this to instruction. I look at standards as the opponents we must face on a yearly basis. As Instructional Leaders, we all understand that most schools do not touch on every standard in a year. We are taught to go deeper not wider. But what if we coached our instructors to find a way to just cover one more standard a year? Or better yet, we created a platform for students to self-lead and assess themselves in standards?

That's one of the framework models we created at my current school. We started with mathematics and have published a book, *"Mastery-Based Mathematics."* We have conducted professional learning with over 70 schools based on the above book. The results are amazing and it boils down to a simple point; you are down one standard at the midpoint of the year but find a way to work smarter. You empower your students to learn that one standard that you may not have time to cover this year.

Starting to Coach in Content Areas. Are You Ready?

The foundation of trust is now set and you are ready to start discussing content. Are you confident in all areas of content? When I began to mentor one of my math educators, for example, I asked a few questions:

1. What do your students struggle with the most?
2. Why do they struggle with that standard so much?
3. Is there anything I can do to help support them?

This questioning took the pressure off of his/her practice and onto the fact that the students were not learning that particular standard. I knew that it was probably an area where the educator struggled or did not have concrete background knowledge on the topic. I immediately began to look for resources. I also asked other math educators how they taught a particular math concept. I looked for professional learning on that topic, as well. Sure enough, I was able to find a local professional learning opportunity that we attended together.

I created the statement, *"If I am going to evaluate you and your practice, I will make sure that I am current in pedagogy and Evidence-Based practices so I can properly evaluate your practice."* This emulated very well with the top educators in the school. When some of the reluctant educators saw that I was willing to learn alongside them, study the current research and listen to PLC ideas on school best practices, more of the educators began to seek out coaching.

Summary

It is so important in a healthy coaching environment you can talk about failures, laugh about them and reflect to understand how as a team, we all can improve. I like to tell educators that making a mistake is how we truly develop best practices for our school. We have found that when educators see co-workers try and implement new strategies on a daily basis, they are far more likely to resist change and attempt implementation. But, when your own educators use Evidence-Based strategies and begin to share the successes and failures, you truly get to see intrinsic motivation toward the improvement in student achievement.

Dr. Tae's, *"Skateboarding Can Save Schools"*, is a great YouTube video that helps all parties realize that failure is okay. Using skateboarding as a means to teach failure is powerful for our learners. If you think about when you first begin to ride a skateboard, you fail much more than you succeed. This video fits well with the Growth Mindset mantra as well as assisting educators and learners with appreciating failure as a means for improvement. I also use another YouTube video called, *"Endo Ethiopia"*, to show educators how to address all the changes coming at us from all directions. It forces the educators to realize we need to simplify our objectives and focus on "one thing" that we can change *now*.

I want to share some quotes that emulate the meaning of this chapter on coaching and provide you inspiration as an Instructional Leader. These quotes can be placed on index cards and you can reflect on them.

Vince Lombardi the Hall of Fame coach states, "Success demands singleness of purpose."

"Remember, success is about doing the right thing, not about doing everything right." Gary Keller

"We are kept from our goal, not by obstacles, but by a clearer path to a lesser goal." Jay Papasan

"People do not decide their future, they decide their habits and their habits decide their future"-Unknown

"A child is one adult away from being a success story." Jack Hunter

"Whatever you allow in August, you will see in May." Unknown

"Knowledge is not power. Knowledge is potential power. Execution is power." Tony Robbins

Now you have read chapters one through five and the puzzle pieces are starting to come together! Continue on your journey!

Chapter 6

Evidence-Based Practices

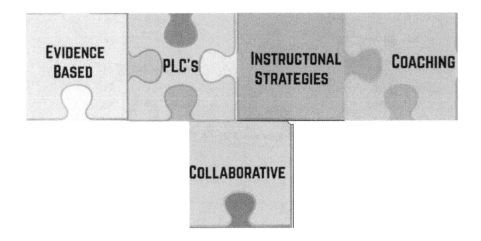

"Things do not grow better; they remain as they are. It is we who grow better, by the changes we make in ourselves." — Swami Vivekananda

Implementing New Evidence-Based Practices

To fully understand Evidence-Based Practices, I looked to the research of John Hattie and Robert Marzano. Both of these educational researchers conducted millions of meta-analysis on what strategies work in classrooms. I was ecstatic after studying the research that four of the five strategies I wanted to implement, both researchers agreed were highly effective. The four strategies Marzano and Hattie agreed upon were: Reciprocal Teaching, Spaced vs. Mass Practice, Microteaching and Jigsaw. The practice that Hattie deemed one of the top ten was the Instructional Strategy of "Jigsaw". This provided added confidence that the strategies I was going to present to staff for implementation would be impactful.

As a review, meta-analysis is true empirical data that changes daily when new validated research is available. In other words, when a research test is completed and deemed reliable, it is added to the meta-analysis. If you look at Hattie's research from 5-7 years ago, you will notice that the effect size of some practices has changed.

I immersed myself in Hattie's and Marzano's work after becoming very frustrated with the lack of proficiency in some of the educator's classrooms. Educators were working very hard teaching but were using strategies that were not as effective as the Evidence-Based Practices previously mentioned.

As an Instructional Leader, I felt it was imperative that we understood what student criteria were for success. The questions we would ask were:

- For instance, what should the learner's academic achievement level be when he/she completes a grade?
- How many standards had the learner mastered?

- How can we pass on the valuable information that was gleaned from the current teacher and ensure it is passed on to next year's educator?

In other words, what does a student need to understand or be proficient in to be deemed successful? The answers to the above questions became our working definition of Success Criteria.

Success Criteria became the foundation for implementing Evidence-Based Practices. Once educators understood Success Criteria and what the learners needed to be proficient in, we had to optimize every aspect of the day to make it as impactful as possible. One way we chose to accomplish this was to only use Evidence-Based Practices in our classrooms. If the research and evidence did not support the practice, it was not suggested to be used in the classroom.

We were creating the image of what our learners should look like in educational terms. I reviewed the research and felt completely proficient in what *effect size* equated to in educational terms. I then was able to articulate what it looked like in practice. In the next sections on Mastery-Based Learning, Reciprocal Teaching, Spaced versus Mass Practice, Microteaching and the Instructional Strategy Jigsaw, these strategies will be fully explained with examples and ideas for implementation. In the next section, I explain the medium that was used to help drive these changes. A dedicated time with educators conversing with educators is paramount for implementing new practices. This type of collaboration has many different abbreviations depending on where you reside, but all have the same framework. I call these practices of teacher collaboration PLCs or Professional Learning Communities.

It is proven that PLCs drive instruction. The leader and leadership team each have a vital role in the implementation of PLCs, the monitoring of PLCs, and assisting the PLCs with implementing the Evidence-Based Practices that are most effective. This provides a great platform for the introduction and learning of these new Evidence-Based Practices inside the PLCs.

PLCs

The term PLCs (Professional Learning Communities) has been around for years and has many different acronyms. PLCs are structured meetings between educators with a definitive goal. This can occur in vertical or horizontal grade bands. The most important component is the conversations that occur in PLCs about improving students' achievement. As an Instructional Leader, it is critical that you stress the importance of communicating across subject areas. Also, the data from these PLC meetings can support the professional learning that is needed at your school.

Professional Learning Communities were created as a means for each group to collaborate and to share best practices. As Dufour writes, "PLCs are not a program. It is a framework of collaborating ideas with stakeholders of the same general grade band." It is very important that as an Instructional Leader, you don't allow the ambiguous notion of discussion drive the time in your PLCs. One example that should take place in PLCs is looking at actual student samples of work compared to a rubric or other samples. You want to ensure that your PLCs are looking at actual student samples of classroom work that the learners have completed. Once you have discussed student work samples in the PLCs, then agree upon what is a high-quality, completed work sample. Base all other assignments off of this representative sample. Discuss, as a group, the strengths of the student samples and the weakness of the samples.

For example, if you notice all students struggling with a specific question on a formative assessment, spend time breaking the question down into parts within your PLC. By completing this portion, the PLC should be able to determine what part of the standard needs to be remediated to ensure student success and mastery. The PLC should not be a regurgitation of information, yet a planning period for any gaps in instruction the data is representing to the PLC group. When a group has become proficient in this practice, it is vital that the PLC group share this information with their peers in other grades. I also suggest each PLC group summarizes their results for the next staff meeting. If you have a PLC that is high-performing and producing results, it is important to allow them to share best practices and model what has worked at a staff meeting as well. As Dufor states, "PLC structure is perpetual!"

Norms of Collaboration

Our school uses some of the adaptive schools' strategies, including the Norms of Collaboration. These adaptive school strategies on collaboration are an excellent framework for PLCs (Professional Learning Communities). **Listed below are the seven steps of collaboration:**

1.   Pausing
2.   Paraphrasing
3.   Posing Questions
4.   Putting Ideas on the Table
5.   Providing Data
6.   Paying Attention to Self and Others
7.   Presuming Positive Intentions

I encourage all PLCs to follow the Norms of Collaboration.

A great resource to use as an Instructional Leader working with PLCs is Austin Buffum's and Mike Matter's, *"It's About Time."* This book gives ideas on how to implement effective intervention time during the school day. Remember, academic environments must rely on school time to impact instruction. We now know, it is the school's responsibility to ensure the students' scholastic needs are met. We need to accept the children for where they are academically, work with them and not accept failure or excuses for students falling behind. In a perfect world, all educators would ensure that prevention is used instead of intervention. In academic settings with high transiency, you must rely on interventions to bring learners to their correct grade level, but also offer above grade-level learners the opportunity to grow.

Teachers may feel they need additional professional learning to increase pedagogy. I noticed with increased professional learning, educators can become easily overwhelmed trying to implement everything they have learned. This causes the focus to be too wide and can lead to educator frustration. As the year begins, I always work with the leadership team to give the PLCs a starting point. Here is the criterion for a PLC meeting:

1. Complete the PLC information form (There are numerous templates on the Internet and in PLC publications).

2. Decide when and where PLCs are going to meet. This must be a consistent day and time so you can schedule to sit in and observe, and offer suggestions as needed (active participant needed).

3. Use your data from the Triangulation Model to create the learning target for the first cycle of the PLC. The data you hope to capture is a pre-test of the skill you noticed was deficient. I have witnessed numerous educators using the pre-test and the post-test and just changing verbiage which is a great idea. This ensures that you are able to accurately gauge the success of your intervention.

4. A typical PLC cycle should encompass around four weeks of instruction with a post assessment determining the success. An example would be if you notice a deficiency in citing text evidence. You could provide a graphic organizer and explicitly instruct the process. You should then notice improvement after four weeks of instruction. The cycle should not take longer, as you are specifically just remediating a specific skill.

How will teachers know if the students need *intervention* or *acceleration*? *Intervention* in our PLCs is defined as, "… working with students who are struggling with current standards or standards from previous grades." *Acceleration* in our PLCs is defined as, "…educators pre-

teaching complex items for deeper understanding."
Accelerated content is instructed to learners who have already met mastery for the standard. The PLCs must look at samples of student work as the means for determining student mastery.

Instructional Leader's Role in PLCs

As an Instructional Leader, it is imperative that you attend as many of the PLC meetings as possible. When you join the meeting, make sure you are an active participant. Your contribution should be supporting staff, offering advice or resources to assist. This also gives you a good pulse of what motivates your staff and the barriers they face in implementing the school's vision. I gain great insight about my staff from attending these PLC meetings. This helps me identify who the teacher leaders are in the group.

I support the growth of educators by conducting learning walk-throughs and sharing my feedback with teachers. I am also able to observe which teachers are working hard and implementing best practices in their instruction. These walk-through practices are paramount to ensure that what you're hearing in the meetings is occurring in the classrooms during daily learning walks.

There are numerous times I visit schools and the principals might be physically present in the PLC meeting, but not mentally present. They have their email open and are not engaged with the topic of the PLC. Attend with an open mind, understand the pulse of the meeting and contribute.

Another critical task is to ensure that your leadership team provides timely feedback to the PLCs. The leadership team should observe and gauge that the PLCs are aligned correctly as well as ensuring they have the necessary resources to perform their tasks. *Alignment* is defined as, "…ensuring that teachers who share students' or content areas, have time to co-plan lessons and also write and design grade level assessments together." Feedback from the administrator helps the PLC grow; however, feedback from peers ensures there is cohesiveness amongst the staff. Depending on your district, you may or may not have funds for before school PLCs or after school PLCs. If those are not options, you need to design the master school schedule with that in mind.

To reiterate, I immerse myself in PLC groups. This is the platform for pedagogical change. I rely on the leadership team to assist with empowering their peers to devise improvement strategies. Educators are more apt to try peer-validated strategies in their classrooms. This becomes a risk-free environment. It is non-evaluative, as the groups consist of peers sharing best practices. This could be something as simple as implementing a new type of formative assessment tool like *Gimkit.* It could be more complex like using *Pear Deck* to flip the classroom. It's a great place for educators to share what they have found to be successful. It is okay if educators discuss Social Emotional Learning ideas as well at this time. However, it is important that the focus be on improvement in academic areas for the majority of the PLCs. When PLCs are meeting, I always attend but do not stay the entire time. My staff understands that I want to visit as many of the PLCs as possible, because normally, more than one meeting occurs on the same day. It is also important that teachers have authentic conversations without an administrator present.

There is an accountability piece with our school PLCs. The educators must provide written documentation of what teaching strategy was discussed and what transpired since the implementation. There are many templates available for PLC documentation and I suggest your leadership team look at the one that fits your school specifically. After these meeting forms are completed, they are emailed to the teacher leader and myself. We disseminate each PLC group's forms as a leadership team to see where support is needed or what is working or not working. It is a very fluid, informal document and the importance of the meetings is teacher collaboration and reviewing of actual student evidence. However, the form is necessary for fidelity of implementation and accountability to the Instructional Leader and teacher leader. Once the document is provided to the Instructional Leader and teacher leader, the document is added to the agenda for the next leadership team meeting. After meeting with the Instructional Leader and leadership team, feedback is provided to each PLC group. This builds a sense of community, as everyone is aware of what strategies and interventions are taking place.

The PLCs inspire a culture of sharing information and Evidence-Based Practices. I prefer PLCs work together in grade-level bands, subject bands, and always include specialists and special education teachers. Specialists are trained in content pedagogy in college, so you can rely on their skill sets, as well. Specialists in most buildings don't have the flexibility to complete interventions at a designated time, as they are normally providing planning for educators. However, I have worked with some schools where specialists have extra duty time or school-wide intervention time. If a specialist has duty time or contractual free time, it is imperative that you match him/her up with an educator or another qualified person to help learners.

I normally will provide a platform for my primary educators to work with specialists and have them assist students with reading. I have found it very beneficial in high schools and middle schools for counselors, specialists and other support staff to work with learners who still struggle with reading or math. This provides the at-risk learner population with another advocate to assist them with remediating the areas where they struggle. Another goal of using support staff in high schools is to provide a support for at-risk learners to assist them with graduation requirements. This can be as simple as helping to monitor their map toward graduation and ensuring they are College and Career ready. Once again, this is something that should be discussed with the leadership team.

We encourage special education teachers to meet as a group and also to meet with their grade-level peers. This allows for sharing of intervention strategies as well as information for behavior management. You will realize that there is much unused capacity in your staff. The majority of the solutions to problems are located right in your building. Creating the platform for risk-free sharing is key to our school improvement.

Simon Sinek states, "When we tell people to do their jobs, we get workers. When we trust people to get the job done, we get leaders." I also like to use the analogy, "Professionals built the Titanic and amateurs built the Arc". Empowering your educators to make decisions and work together as a staff creates scalable leadership. This is needed if you are going to focus on Shared Leadership as an Instructional Leader. It is difficult for some principals to get out of his/her office to visit a classroom. By empowering educators to assist with the leadership of the school, you will have more time for instruction.

I am often asked by mentees what are the best questions to ask in PLCs to stimulate conversation. As always, there are a plethora of questions, but here are a few I like to use for specific reasons:

1. What do you think about it? (This is open-ended and allows the educator a platform for stating his/her perceptions and ideas) *Adverse: "Do you believe in...?"*

2. Would you consider it? (This is another great question when you are trying to accomplish having an educator make a small change) *Adverse: "Why don't you...?"*

3. What does it look like when...?" (This is a great self-reflection piece for groups to discuss. This works very well when conducting micro-teaching exercises.) *Adverse: "What will happen if...?"*

4. What might you learn from this? (Great when talking about professional learning) *Adverse: "What did you think would happen?" "What's up with...?"*

5. What evidence do you have? (This is a great way to pose a question when you are trying to challenge a specific idea or thought of an educator or group of educators.) *Adverse: "What is wrong with...?"*

6. What am I missing? (This question shows humility and also allows the people you are working with to see that

you care about their thoughts and want their input.)
Adverse: "Does everyone agree with me"?

These are just a few examples of questions that can be asked to help guide deep conversations that will lead to rich discussions in PLCs. When a more straightforward approach is needed, I rely on the work of Ray Dalio, the investment banker. He tells his leaders and managers, "It's a fundamental law of nature that in order to gain strength, one has to push one's limits, which is painful." Most people avoid the pain and rely on complacency because it feels "okay". They might change one small habit, but it takes immense conversations from peers, leaders and yourself to finally encourage people to face the harsh reality that they are not as impactful as they perceive themselves to be. As I have said numerous times, "Unless you would feel comfortable putting your own child in a specific teacher's class, why is it alright for another child to have an inferior educator?"

In conclusion of this section on PLCs, I wanted to share with you that PLCs have numerous opportunities for implementation of new strategies. The main strategy that I used to drive PLC growth and improve leadership capacity was Hattie's idea of Collective Efficacy. Hattie defines *Collective Efficacy* as "...teachers' shared belief through collective action can positively influence student outcomes, including impacting those who are disengaged or disadvantaged."

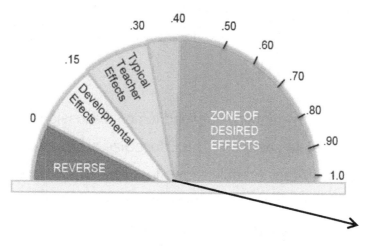

Collective Efficacy Effect Size 1.57

Hattie, J. (2009). *Visible learning: A synthesis of over 800 meta-analyses related to achievement.* New York: Routledge.

I believe that Collective Efficacy is paramount. Improvement occurs when the administrator is responsive to teacher needs and encouraging teacher collaboration through PLCs. PLCs are not a time for educators to grade papers or make copies. Having one of your teacher leaders in each PLC ensures time is spent with fidelity. Compliance is important and needed, but your teacher leaders will also keep you abreast of issues that present themselves in each PLC meeting.

As an Instructional Leader, you should continue to push the message in PLCs that it is less about "how to teach" and more about the "impact of teaching".

- What does it mean to be good at Algebra One?
- What is the criterion for success for a student who earns an "A" in Algebra One?
- Are the learners consistent?
- What does it look like to show one year's growth in music or choir?

These conversations can lead to rich discussions that can yield immediate changes. The Effect Size above of the Collective Efficacy graphic shows that when educators collaborate, positive outcomes occur in student learning.

Here is a chart of the five strategies that will be discussed in this chapter. I have provided a column discussing which Evidence-Based Practice John Hattie and Robert Marzano agree are high impact strategies. In each section, I will provide insight into implementation ideas, impactful evidence and a process for ongoing success.

Strategy	Effect Size	Marzano/Hattie Agree	HS/MS/ K-6
Mastery-Based Learning	1.79	No	ALL
Microteaching	.88	Yes	ALL
Reciprocal Teaching	.74	Yes	ALL
Spaced vs. Mass Practice	.82	Yes	ALL
Jigsaw	1.20	No	No

As you can tell from the above practices, they all account for more than one year's growth in one year's time. As a refresher, the average student growth equates to .4, which is one year's growth.

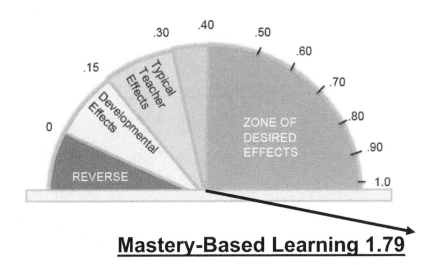

Mastery-Based Learning 1.79

Hattie, J. (2009). *Visible learning: A synthesis of over 800 meta-analyses related to achievement.* New York: Routledge.

The first practice I will share is Mastery-Based Learning, which has an effect size of 1.79. As I stated earlier, we were showing growth as a school, but not enough to make up the tremendous learning gaps, especially in mathematics. I spent three months deciphering Evidence-Based practices and reviewing our mathematical data. This motivated me to continue to find or develop a framework to improve our learners' academics, especially in mathematics. Knowing that our learners were behind academically in mathematics, as an Instructional Leader, I broke down the schoolwide state summative math data. I could see as a school we were not meeting the needs of every student in math. The traditional mathematics instruction we were providing our learners were working, however, not fast enough and not on a scalable basis. Mastery allows each learner opportunities to excel in mathematics, regardless of their starting point.

I created the following message and facilitated the implementation of Evidence-Based Practices. The phrase I use as my Instructional Leader statement for growth is that we strive to achieve, "...more than one year's growth in one year's time". I knew that traditional methods and even vetted strategies could not alleviate the multiple year gaps that my learners had in mathematics. This sparked the advent of Mastery-Based Mathematics. I created this strategy one summer when I was deciding which strategy to implement for mathematical school improvement. The Mastery-Based Learning strategy can be used in any and all content areas because it is an Evidence-Based Practice. However, our mathematical data was significantly below the district and state norms and needed immense improvement. Therefore, I implemented a Mastery-Based Learning Framework and refer to it as Mastery-Based Learning in Mathematics. I created this framework based on self-reporting grades, Spaced vs Mass practice and feedback. This process encompassed all of the above strategies and also included a tracking system for formative assessments. Mastery-Based Mathematics relies heavily upon student intrinsic motivation and the educators instructing as coaches and cheerleaders.

Once I felt empowered with the research and created the framework, I asked one of my trailblazer educators to implement this practice as a pilot. I knew I had to get teacher buy-in before I could ask the leadership team to implement this framework school-wide. Once the educator implemented the framework, we began to see results instantly. The students were as equally excited as the educator. We began to celebrate the success. This framework created the desire for other educators to implement the strategy. _This allowed the strategy to grow organically without being mandated._

The pilot educator and I worked on creating leveled assessments while also ensuring learners were motivated. This meant I was not only coaching the educator, but also coaching the learners. I was in the classroom observing and participating in the math excitement. Much to our surprise and excitement, 100% of learners passed the state assessment test in mathematics that year. The scores for this class on the state mathematics assessment were higher than the state average. In the previous four years, the scores never rose above 60% on mathematics state assessments. This truly was a game changer. We celebrated this accomplishment as a school and other educators became increasingly interested in the success of this implementation. Excitingly, six other educators adapted Mastery-Based learning the next year and the results were amazing, as well. On average, the scores on the state math assessments improved by 40-50% in one year. We are changing the math aptitude of dozens of cohorts of learners by simply changing one practice.

This has worked so well that I have consulted with

numerous high schools, middle schools and elementary schools because this is a proven successful framework. Schools contact and request us to share with their math educators what we are doing to remarkably improve our mathematics summative state test scores. One of the local high schools I consult saw their algebra one scores improve 28% in one year. This required a commitment from algebra one educators and the school leadership to embrace this type of mathematical pedagogical change. This high school went from teaching content to specifically teaching the standards to the strength and weaknesses of the learners. As we delved into algebra one, there were dozens and dozens of standards that needed to be covered. This was overwhelming for educators. We broke down the standards into power standards and first focused on how many power standards we could anticipate the learners to master. Most learners achieved level one in the power standards and a good portion, level two (levels will be explained in section *What is the Practice?*) We also noticed the intrinsic motivation for learners to want to improve in the areas where they were strongest.

In the next section, I will discuss implementation of Mastery-Based Mathematics. The results of this framework solidified the research and validated the effect sizes that we anticipated. Once this framework solidified success, it catapulted a pilot educator and I to write a book on Mastery-Based Mathematics. The book has been extremely well received by educators at all teaching levels. We currently consult with dozens of schools and have provided professional learning at numerous conferences on this successful mathematics framework.

What Is the Mastery-Based Mathematics Practice?

It is the creation of an assessment system where students are able to work at their own pace developing their strengths. For instance, when giving pre-assessments, we are able to locate the strengths our learners have in specific standards. Instead of waiting for that topic to be covered in math class, we allow students to self-pace and report their scores on the standards they recently learned.

For example, we had a student with disabilities who struggled with division in 8th grade mathematics, but was amazing in geometry. We instructed that learner to complete the leveled mastery assignments in geometry to show mastery. This not only built confidence, it enabled him/her to go deeper in a strength area of the content. All learners chart mastered standards on mastery charts. We developed three specific levels of mastery. These levels are not based on DOK (Depth of Knowledge) skills, but on conceptual understanding.

Level One: Assessment is your basic algorithmic type of problem. We expect all of our learners to be able to accomplish these assessments after the concept is taught. This includes our students with disabilities.

Level Two: Assessments consist of your State Assessments, such as PARCC, Smarter Balance, AIR and other state-approved assessments. We use sample and released questions on each standard to deem students proficient. This data provides insight for the educator and administration on passage rates on future high stakes assessments. This is excellent data to bring to PLCs when you are using the Triangulation Model. It is also important for Instructional Leaders to add this data to your data wall and spreadsheets. This way, everyone can visually see and predict where the students are proficient in each standard.

Level Three: Assessments consist of projects that show application of the standard. For instance, some of our high school learners have created carnival games with probability standards, geometry golf courses and other items that show true mastery and application of standards. Be aware, not every one of your students will reach this level and very rarely will any learner reach level three on all standards, even at the high school level. Due to the vast number of standards at the high school level, we look specifically at mastery of the power standards in mathematics. This ensures high school students have knowledge of the content needed to graduate and will also score well on the SAT and ACT or ACT Works.

When Is Mastery-Based Mathematics Implemented?

Mastery-Based Mathematics needs to be implemented during the summer with an educator or two at a specific grade level. This is not a strategy in itself, but more of a framework with multiple strategies embedded. This framework will yield more than one year's growth in one year's time, guaranteed. I have worked with over 30 schools and not one school has experienced math growth below 20% in the grade they implemented this framework and process. Once you have selected the grade to implement, ensure you provide ample time during the year for creation of assessments or to locate the assessments agreed upon by standard. For mastery to occur, a pre-test and post-test must be available. There must also be at least three different versions of assessment for each standard. These can be teacher created, or at the minimum, provide time and resources for educators to find and vet assessments for mastery.

During the first year of implementation, this should be the only new task for these educators. To ensure this framework is implemented with fidelity, it is important the educators who are implementing this framework are not tasked with implementing other programs as well. They should be looking at student assessment samples as well as using PLC time to collaborate on grouping of students. These groups establish where students need remediation or acceleration.

To clarify, the educator instructs his/her normal curriculum Monday through Thursday, while on Fridays they conduct Math Mastery Days. The sole purpose is for the educator to assess the students' scores from the week's math instruction. Educators allow learners to self-report and self-assess areas where they have worked independently or already have content knowledge. Educators can also use *Khan Academy* or create separate videos by standard to allow students to work ahead or self-remediate. Students record their strengths and struggles. This practice is robust which is why an entire book is dedicated to *Mastery-Based Learning in Mathematics*.

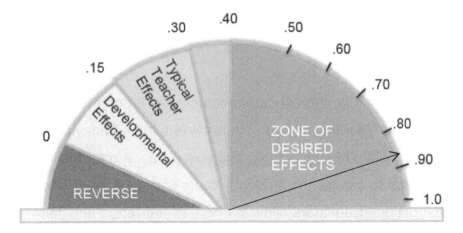

Microteaching .88

Hattie, J. (2009). *Visible learning: A synthesis of over 800 meta-analyses related to achievement.* New York: Routledge.

The next strategy I will discuss is Microteaching, which has an effect size of .88. This term has been in the educational realm since 1963 and has taken numerous definitions. You can Google it and find a plethora of videos, charts and other resources to see if there are anomalies that work better for your organization. Microteaching is not a new practice. It has been vetted since its first creation in Japan as the Japanese Study Model. The adaptation of this model to the United States has been well received and has a multiple year growth potential as a practice. The above chart is taken from John Hattie's research; however, Marzano is also a firm believer in the impact of the Microteaching strategy.

What Is the Microteaching Practice?

The focus of this strategy is to allow an educator the opportunity to illicit feedback on the teaching of a specific skill or process. In traditional settings, this is required in pre-service classes for teaching degrees. We use this process of Microteaching in PLCs, as it creates a more authentic learning opportunity.

Step 1: The educator plans a lesson to be taught to either a small group or whole group. When it is taught to a small group, the process works more fluidly. By using small groups, the process is able to be streamlined and the educator is able to improve upon feedback when it is taught to another small group of the same class. The lesson should consist of no more than approximately twenty minutes. We use the "I DO, We DO, You DO" gradual release model in our school. Our normal Microteaching occurs during the "I DO" portion of the lesson which is about fifteen to twenty minutes or shorter/longer, depending on the age/grade level.

Step 2: The lesson is recorded and played for his/her PLC group at the next meeting. The educator explains what he/she noticed (self-reflection), and then each observing educator is required to provide one reinforcement and one refinement to the educator.

Step 3: The lesson can be discussed as part of the feedback process (The Norms of Collaboration should be followed and the conversations should remain on the topics of one reinforcement and one refinement). Feedback is meant to build up the educator's pedagogy and self-reflection with peers, leading to improved educator performance.

Step 4: Educator replans after reflecting on the feedback provided by the PLC.

Step 5: He/She reteaches the lesson to another small group of learners and records his/her lesson. He/she then self-reflects and decides if he/she wants feedback on this section or he/she can decide to just self-reflect. In our school, most educators want the feedback after the second recording of the lesson. However, it is perfectly fine to just self-assess or share with one trusted educator or critical friend.

Step 6: Feedback. This would be the second round of feedback, and as I mentioned above, it can occur through self-reflection, PLCs or with a critical or trusted peer.
Here is a flowchart we use as guidance for Microteaching in our PLCs.

Microteaching Flowchart Process

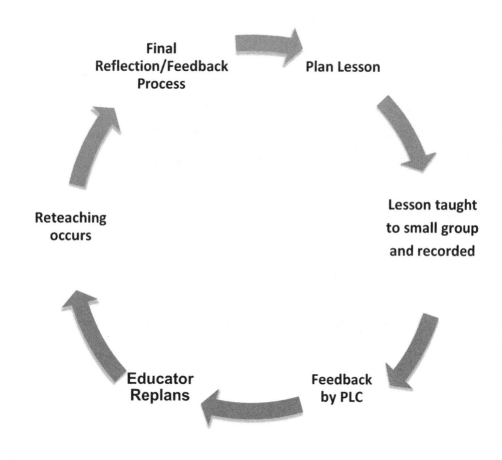

When Is Microteaching Implemented?

I would highly recommend the implementation of Microteaching occur in the first quarter of a school year. I would select the PLC group with the strongest educators who are also open to feedback. Once this Microteaching practice has proven successful, it is time to share the success of the strategy with others. Look for school-wide implementation in the 2nd and 3rd quarter of the school year. Once it has been implemented, it should become commonplace in PLC meetings. As you add new initiatives, it is easy for this type of practice to fall by the wayside. One way we keep it relevant is by having educators record the first three minutes or last three minutes of a lesson. This allows the group to provide feedback on formative assessments and also share best practices. We know the two most impactful parts of a lesson is the beginning and the end.

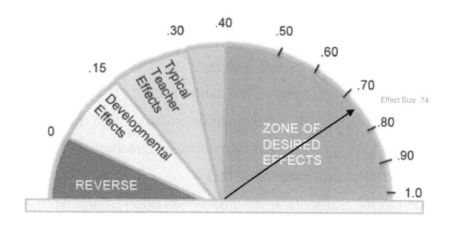

<u>Reciprocal Teaching   .74</u>

The third strategy I will introduce is Reciprocal Teaching which has an effect size of .74. *Reciprocal Teaching* practice is explained as: "A teaching strategy that assists educators to effectively implement the type of close, evidence-based reading called for in any standards-based curriculum, including the Common Core State Standards." With an increase in both informational texts and more rigorous reading material, students need Reciprocal Teaching now more than ever to help them comprehend. Since Reciprocal Teaching is a discussion technique, many listening and speaking standards are naturally met.

Each of these four strategies of Reciprocal Teaching plays an important role in meeting a variety of standards. The four strategies are *predicting, questioning, clarifying* and *summarizing*. They are explained in detail below:

- Predict: Students make predictions using evidence from the text, such as text features. Students also predict the author's purpose and text organization.
- Question: Students cite textual evidence and draw on multiple sources to ask and answer questions in order to better understand the text.
- Clarify: Students apply grade-level phonics and word analysis skills to decode new and unfamiliar words. They rely on context to confirm, self-correct, and reread when necessary. They also analyze how parts of the text fit together and clarify by rereading or reading on to figure out confusing points, words, or phrases.
- Summarize: Students identify main ideas and details, then compare and contrast the structure of a text to determine themes and summarize narrative text. They also integrate and evaluate information from the text and support their claims with text evidence. This is a high-level skill.

You will see according to John Hattie's Meta-Analysis, Reciprocal Teaching has an effect size of .74. Now, the nice thing about his research is that it is always changing. The effect size could move slightly, depending on the research he is still accumulating, to prove the strategies he analyses are continually validated. Using Hattie's research, I encourage all aspiring and seasoned Instructional Leaders to become granularly familiar with an average year's growth for a student as .4. If educators use Reciprocal Teaching correctly in their content area, they can basically expect two full years of growth. Imagine Reciprocal Teaching implemented in all content areas! That's why, as a school, we selected Reciprocal Teaching as a game changer to improve the comprehension skills and critical thinking skills of our learners.

What Is the Reciprocal Teaching Practice?

The educator takes a grade-level passage (short read) no more than a one or two page article. He/She breaks the passage into sections. An example would consist of breaking large paragraphs into smaller paragraphs to ensure everyone has a part to read. In most groups, each learner is assigned more than one piece of the text. This ensures that each group member has a chance to read multiple times. The students are split into groups of no more than five.

Step One: Pass out the passage to each person. The educator should be the leader for the first 2-3 lessons to ensure the "teacher", when assigned, understands the role. When the Reciprocal Teaching process is fully understood, it should be student led.

The teacher asks, "Before you begin to read the selection, look at the main title, scan the page or pages and look at major illustrations. Do not read specific sentences, just look at headings." When you have finished, write down your prediction or share what you think the story or article will cover. This should take no more than 1-2 minutes.

Step Two: Select a learner in the group to read the next section or paragraph. When finished reading, have everyone in the group summarize the main idea of the paragraph or section. These summaries should then be shared (I have seen it completed where the teacher waits until the end to share the main idea. This is fine. This strategy is very adaptive).

Step Three: Have each person write down one question that the main idea will answer. Direct your learners to use words like; who, where, when, why and what. This should be completed for each paragraph or section that students read.

Step Four: As the reader is reading their section, have the group members who are struggling with understanding a word, highlight or underline the word they do not understand. When the section is completed, the teacher or leader should ask if there are any words that need clarification. Then, as a group, they share the meaning using context clues, background information, or online tools to confirm.

<u>Step Five:</u> There is no need for additional assessment, as once the learners are working in their groups, the educator is managing by proximity and assessing as they are completing the activity. We have used various formative assessment tools, such as; checklists, look for's, and quick exit tickets.

When Is Reciprocal Teaching Implemented?

It is imperative to have professional learning for the entire school staff prior to implementation. There are numerous videos on "The Teaching Channel" which will assist educators. We fortunately have an educator who is well versed in Reciprocal Teaching and provided the professional learning for the staff. Once the staff received the initial professional learning, I asked them to attempt it during one class. I was so amazed! Everyone was so excited they tried it the first week. The feedback was astounding. This practice became a staple at my school and is a strategy that has improved reading and Evidence-Based collection across all content areas.

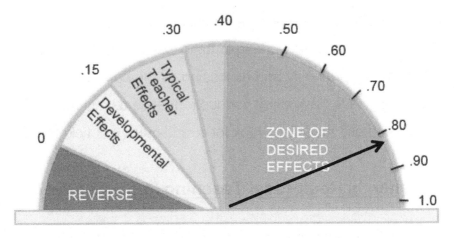

Spaced Versus Mass Practice .82

Hattie, J. (2009). *Visible learning: A synthesis of over 800 meta-analyses related to achievement.* New York: Routledge.

The fourth strategy I would like to share is Spaced versus Mass Practice which has an effect size of .82.

What Is the Spaced Versus Mass Practice Strategy?

Mass Practice is concentrated practice with short-term satisfaction. Spaced Practice is practice spread out over several sessions with long-term understanding and transfer. For the majority of our strategies, we calculate our own effect size to ensure the practice fits our demographics. In some studies, I have seen this practice have an effect size of .62 and I have seen it as high as .84. As we know with meta-analysis, the more the practice is researched, the closer the data comes to a consensus. We calculated our own effect size for this practice and came to an effect size of .80, well within the range of the other studies. Both rationale and process is to provide learners with various opportunities to practice a specific skill.

How Is Spaced Versus Mass Practice Implemented?

Instead of just giving one whole class period to rotate through the skills (work on a skill and then moving to the next skill), Spaced versus Mass Practice creates opportunities for re-assessment on an ongoing basis. The mastery model described in the previous section incorporates this practice immensely. However, if mastery is not a chosen practice by your school, this practice Spaced versus Mass Practice is highly encouraged to implement. This process is very similar to "looping". You instruct and assess and then, over the course of the standard, you continually offer activities for the learner to answer questions on previously taught concepts. Spaced versus Mass Practice is a strategy that should be incorporated at a minimum, weekly. By doing so, it will ensure that semester and final exams, as well as quarterly assessments, allow the learner's time to demonstrate proficiency. By continually revisiting and reassessing, you are gauging the transfer of content knowledge that occurred on the concepts that were instructed. It also allows the learner to understand his/her strengths and weaknesses.

Here is a visual flowchart of how we use Spaced versus Mass Practice to guide transfer:

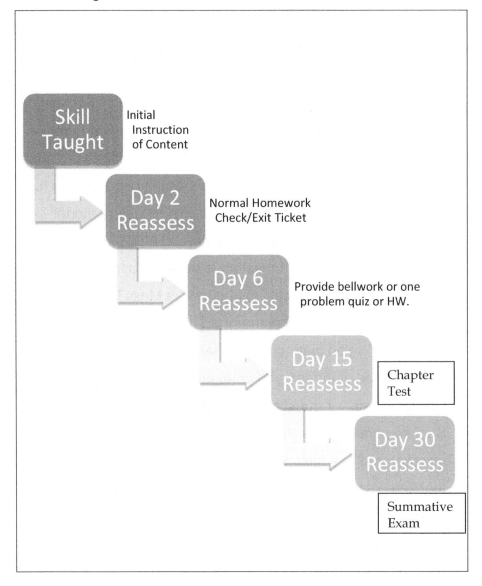

When Is Spaced Versus Mass Practice Implemented?

The leadership team and I presented this Spaced versus Mass Practice strategy to our math educators at a staff meeting. We asked them to work together in their PLCs to come up with some ideas for implementation. This practice was embraced quickly. It is an impactful strategy that did not require a change of practice other than more frequent assessments on past instructed standards. I suggest this strategy as one of the first practices to ask your educators to embrace. This is extremely beneficial at the high school level where educators are concerned about covering content. The training for this strategy is nominal. Educators know the content which will ensure this practice requires minimal changes. Educators can focus on creating simple formative checks. It also provides a great place for educator reflection. It allows the educator to ensure transfer takes place, ensuring the content was covered thoroughly.

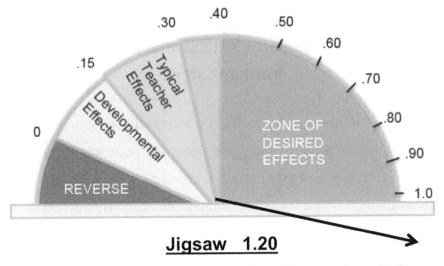

Jigsaw 1.20

Hattie, J. (2009). *Visible learning: A synthesis of over 800 meta-analyses related to achievement.* New York: Routledge.

The fifth strategy I would like to introduce is the Jigsaw Strategy which has an effect size of 1.20. This strategy has a very high effect size and when used correctly, helps to promote deep rich conversations and enhance the transfer of content. To use the Jigsaw method below the fourth grade level would take scaffolding on the part of the educator. However, in middle school and high school, this is a very powerful strategy that engages all learners and also incorporates numerous other strategies.

What Is the Jigsaw Strategy?

Jigsaw is a technique or method of organizing a classroom that makes students dependent on each other to succeed. It breaks a class into groups and breaks assignments into pieces. The groups then put the pieces together. The Jigsaw Strategy incorporates critical thinking skills, social skills, as well as listening, communication and problem-solving skills. Numerous educators have completed "Jigsaw techniques" in college or may even use them currently in their classroom. That is fantastic! As an Instructional Leader, you want to praise those educators for using an Evidence-Based Practice that improves student achievement. I would challenge you if this practice is widespread in your school to conduct a staff meeting using the Jigsaw strategy.

As an Instructional Leader, utilizing this strategy at staff meetings will assist educators with understanding how much student or adult engagement assists with implementing practices. In classrooms where these strategies are prevalent, apathy is at a minimum and engagement is always a focal point.

How Is Jigsaw Implemented?

There are numerous steps when setting up a Jigsaw. However, once your learners get used to the process, there is fluidity to it.

Step One: Divide your learners into heterogeneous groups with five or six learners in each. Varying ability levels is also encouraged.

Step Two: Select one learner to be the leader for this activity (Ensure you are fair and rotate as you complete more Jigsaws).

Step Three: Divide the lesson or content into sections so each learner has a section. Some examples are: characteristics of different rocks, study history of Abraham Lincoln (break apart his childhood, triumphs, failures, rise to presidency, legacy, etc.).

Step Four: Assign each segment to a learner (This should be teacher driven).

Step Five: Provide ample time for students to cold read and reread to better understand the topic.

Step Six: Have all the students assigned to the same section of the assignment form a group. Students then discuss what they each felt was most valuable and what they believe should be taught to the rest of the class. Give 5-7 minutes to practice and discuss.

Step Seven: Have learners return to original group. Next, have them present as the leader of their individual sections. The Jigsaw strategy is very powerful, as they are summarizing the most important agreed upon concepts from step six. This is a great way to get the "gist" of complex texts and also have multiple reads.

Step Eight: Educators should be circulating, checking for understanding and on-task behavior. At the end of the activity, it is important to have some type of assessment. This could be online such as a *Kahoot* or *Create a Quiz* in Google Forms. Immediate feedback is important!

When Is Jigsaw Strategy Implemented?

This particular strategy can be implemented once the staff is trained. As an Instructional Leader, this is a perfect opportunity for you to lead professional learning on the Jigsaw strategy. Create a *simple poster board or chart showing* the steps and lead your staff through a Jigsaw. If you simply

Google, Jigsaw, you will find entire sites and books on the practice. We found it simple to implement and each educator used their own "version" of it to ensure it met the needs of their learners. The foundation of the Jigsaw practice was still the same, regardless of how the educator scaffolded it for his/her learners. The impact of Jigsaw on formative assessments has proven that this effect size works in schools.

Summary

After years of intense research on John Hattie and his successful data research on effect size, I took seven of my leadership team members to a John Hattie 3-day conference. At the conference, we spent time planning on what school-wide strategies we were going to adopt. After each session, we spent a few minutes digressing the information we gained. We each were responsible for taking detailed notes and sharing out as a group to ensure we maximized the amount of learning that could occur. We made an abundance of decisions to be implemented for the following year at that conference. This was a pivotal moment and one in which we developed excellent collective efficacy.

The educators were so excited to attend the conference, as they were aware that Hattie's and Marzano's work was the foundation for the framework of Mastery-Based Learning in Mathematics. They were eager to see what other strategies could be implemented at our school to help other content areas excel as well.

In addition to adopting this strategy for math, we adopted Reciprocal Teaching and agreed to focus on providing feedback to our students. With Mastery-Based Learning in Mathematics, and Reciprocal Teaching across all content areas, we had more than enough new initiatives to implement the following year. I was there coaching and learning, alongside staff, while they were planning to change their practice.

We were recently rated the number one urban school in the state. We were nominated as a National School to Watch, a Momentum Award Winner and State School to Watch. This is in addition to other local and state-wide awards. This is a success story, as we previously were rated an "F" school in numerous categories. This proves *Instructional Leadership utilizing Coaching works!*

John Hattie's publications are very diverse and broken down into multiple subjects. Do not expect your staff to improve in all areas in a year. When I work with high schools, I encourage them to select one practice per subject area. When I work with elementary and middle school educators, I lean them toward one practice in math and one in reading. The one practice I always encourage is using Reciprocal Teaching in content areas. This practice is one that Marzano and Hattie agree is high performing. In my building,

Reciprocal Teaching is used in ELA, Science, and Social Studies and I have witnessed tremendous growth.

As John Hattie says, "There is no such thing as a bad teacher, there are just more effective ones." I truly keep that mindset when I am working with reluctant educators, or educators who struggle with classroom management or implementation of practice. Keep this in mind, as you are coaching and assisting educators with implementing Evidence-Based Practices.

Once you are able to get educators to commit to their own learning and they understand the objectives as realistic and attainable, they start to make immediate changes to their pedagogy and practice. Educators need to see that these strategies are applicable to their daily routine and can be implemented with support from each other and the lead learner.

An important key point I learned while spending time coaching and working with different levels of educators is professional learning does not automatically transfer into practice. The educators need to have a platform for deep rich conversation with peers on the implementation. Don't be fooled by sending teachers to professional learning and thinking that is the silver bullet. It must be intentional and you, as the Instructional Leader, must create the platform for sharing the professional learning amongst each member of the staff. So many mentees tell me they send teachers to professional learning and they never see it implemented. You have to make sure your leadership team helps guide you in selecting which educators are ready for more professional learning. Once others in your building see that implementation can happen and they have your support and the support of teacher leaders, they feel more empowered to help themselves. This, in turn, yields higher student achievement. **Everything you do as an Instructional Leader has to yield positive change in student performance!**

Frequently Asked Questions by Mentees

Q: How do you motivate educators?

A: A question often asked by leaders I am mentoring is how I motivate educators who seem uninterested in perfecting their craft. I mentioned earlier that not all educators will trust in you as an Instructional Leader. However, I want to provide a more straightforward approach for dealing with reluctant educators who appear to be there as a "job". You will find success if around 20% of your staff is not on board. If you believe you have around 60% or more of your staff on board with your leadership, here are some strategies for handling conversations. It is important that you engage in conversations with the correct frame of mind. I was told a Native American Story a long time ago by a wise man. He stated, "Each of us has two wolves inside of you. A vicious and competitive wolf and a kind and loving wolf. The wolves inside are constantly battling for superiority. The one that wins is the one that you feed."

The morale I got from this story is that as a leader you cannot let others dictate your communication style. If you have the mindset of humility and your sole purpose is to improve the lives of the students in your building and community, your loci (focus) will never wane.

This is the main reason why I have all aspiring Instructional Leaders start with their personal vision statement.

Q: Are Evidence-Based Practices prevalent in any other areas of society?

A: Evidence-Based practices have been utilized in medicine and businesses for a long time and it is encouraging that educational institutions are starting to adapt that mindset. Through the most current brain research, we know that decisions are sometimes made subconsciously or parts of the brain are hijacked by other parts. There are numerous publications that are relevant to our profession on brain research. John Medina, "Brain Rules", is a very good read with application toward education. I would also encourage everyone to read Ray Dalio's book "*Principles*". It relates to wealth building, but the lessons contained are relevant to situations in life and situations we deal with on a day to day basis. Remember growth and learning can occur in all places not just in educational institutions or educational publications. Most of the lessons that impacted me were conversations that transpired when I was not looking to be impacted. Learn from everyone you come in contact with. As you continue on your educational journey, when you read publications, they provide the "evidence and affirmation that what you are doing has a chance for success."

Q: How do Community Partners assist with Student Achievement?

A: When I look back on the economic and human capital impact that volunteers and corporate relationships have on my school's success, it was hard to imagine how I did it without all the volunteers and corporate relationships. Before I went ahead and started corporate partnership, I worked with my leadership team and provided the evidence that adult tutoring has an effect size of .28. This is not very high, but if scheduled correctly could enhance the learning of students who were struggling. I began to approach businesses. I asked for capital to fund computer based intervention programs promising them the use with fidelity. I also wanted to communicate to the donors how their donations impacted student growth. Once these partnerships proved to be successful I began to ask companies/churches that are not able to donate financially to invest with volunteers. I was surprised how many companies allowed their employees the freedom to take their lunch time and work with students. The leadership team agreed that the effect size would show impact and we began the mentoring program that currently enlists over 80 weekly mentors. This is a large endeavor and one in which I own personally.

Q: Who manages the Volunteer Program at your school?

A: Some people wonder why I choose to manage the volunteer program personally. The reason is because it deals with people who are giving up their time to invest in the lives of the students. In essence, volunteers are helping to uncover the hidden talents in our students. In addition, the College and Career Readiness portion of the conversations are invaluable. Our students get to work with industry professionals, ask questions and learn about various local and national careers. It is a huge win for the mentors and the mentees. For more specific information please feel free to contact me.

Q: So how do you approach a large company when they get inundated with people looking for philanthropic handouts?

A: Here are a few options:
1. Visit your local rotary club meeting and present your proposal
2. Ask your superintendent who he/she knows locally that you need to get to know to help the school.
3. Cold Call
4. Use Linkedin

Q: Do you have any ineffective teachers at your school?

A: When John Hattie's work first came into educational realms we all learned that if a student was in a school with a teacher he/she would show growth just by being in school doing some type of work. This has been vetted and debated through educational circles and through his meta-analysis we know it to be true. He further goes on to state there are no such thing as bad educator's only more effective ones. If you focus on Instructional Leadership and provide the instructional strategies I have provided you; you will notice immense improvement in your educator capacity.

Q: How do you manage time when dealing with people?

A: Leaders that I mentor are always amazed how much work I can accomplish in a single day or school year. They often ask me if I sleep. The answer is absolutely. I work on the most impactful practices that produce the most impact for the teachers, students and families I serve. There are plenty of things that could be delegated during the school day that yield very little impact on the school and student achievement. In Chapter Two you will have a time management activity to complete which will help you determine which are the most impactful decisions you make with your time each day. This will hopefully provide you with the insight to delegate the correct items allowing you time to focus on educational initiatives that lead to improved student achievement. John Maxwell explains it very well with this quote "What I value is what I find time for". If you value having coffee and talking in the morning you will make sure that you find time for that. If you value working with kids in classrooms you will find time for that. I choose to conduct business as if my students are my clients and my goal is to provide them with the best education possible. To truly understand what the students are learning you have to become a data master, classroom walkthrough master, small group learning master and communication master. Yes, I used the word master as this is a huge part of Instructional Leadership. If you understand where the kids are academically you can provide support for educators. As you become engrossed and proficient on walk-throughs and communication with your educators you will notice that you have a better pulse on the educational needs of your school. This is extremely relevant as you are the Instructional Leader and you have to be able to foresee struggles and also curtail them before the struggle occurs. You become a systems thinker!

Q: How do you ensure you make the right decisions for your organization?

A: As the Instructional Leader, every decision you make, regardless if it shared or not, is your responsibility. This decision-making process should occur prior to the ideas being presented to the leadership team. This is your time to pre-select what you believe is in the best interest of your school.

Step One: Does the idea or issue relate to the school's vision statement? If an educator brings an academic issue or academic problem, it is imperative that you make a decision on whether it is important enough to bring to your leadership team. There are numerous times that problems or ideas are brought to me. I filter out and investigate the ideas to ensure they are aligned to our vision.

Step Two: Gather the evidence to support whether this item is Evidence-Based. Can we create our own data or calculate effect size if it is a new process? Collect as much information as you can if you believe this idea could possibly be implemented to help drive student achievement.

Step Three: Identify any alternatives you come across while researching whether this program, idea or solution has other alternatives. Sometimes when solving a problem, you come across multiple solutions or something else that solved the problem in its entirety. If you identify an alternative, follow the same process as you did with the original idea.

Step Four: Collate any evidence that supports the program or idea to move forward to the leadership team. This is a key step when you bring an idea to your team. It should already have met the above criteria and the staff should look at the nuts and bolts of the program, process or ideas. The team should not have to spend time trying to find information on the process; it should all be done prior to the meeting. You are the Instructional Leader and the power is in deciding what items are brought to the leadership team.

Step Five: Take action and present the idea to the leadership team. Whenever possible, have the educator who brought you the idea or product present and explain any background knowledge or research in order to create consensus. Be sure to include any information gathered from other educators who have already used it etc. For example, has the idea or product ever been used by other educators in the building? If so, what were the results? Where is the data to support implementation?

Step Six: Reflect on the decision prior to implementation. Review the decision the leadership team has made and if you still concur, **keep doing, stop doing, delegate doing** put it into action using the implementation timeline you and the leadership team created.

"Instructional Leadership is measured daily. It is not a culmination of items you have been successful with over the years."

Q: How do you handle educators who produce positive student achievement scores but do not get involved in anything else?

A: First off you must respect the educator who comes to work on time, and follows the rules and works hard, but just chooses not to enlist in leadership opportunities or become part of leadership. Every school has those educators who perform well yet prefer to work independently and the majority of the time they are successful. These educators are respected, but will not form the core of your leadership and will not move the school to the next level. These educators are people who will follow the rules and framework, but will not be quick to reinvent their practice. The more educators you have in your organization that believes in your vision, the fewer people there are against your vision. One of the key traits that some leaders take for granted is treasuring honorable people in his or her organization. These are the people, for example, that treat you well when you are not looking. They are rare and you must ensure they are treated well and are honored. They help ensure the positive culture continues to improve.

Q: You mention calculating your own effect size for Mastery-Based Learning. How did you compute this and is there a formula?

A: That is a fabulous question and one I am asked quite often when presenting. I always start with the question of what is good data. Using summative state assessments and the quarterly assessments are a great way to calculate effect sizes. I never try to calculate an effect size of a practice unless it has been implemented for at least 3 months. With Mastery-Based Learning it was over a 9 month period. The role of this data of this data dissemination is to assist educators with development of the Evidence-Based Practices that were selected to be implemented. It should not be used for evaluation at the school level. I calculated effect sizes three different ways and then averaged them to ensure the effect size I broadcasted was accurate. I checked effect size of top students, struggling students and the whole group as a whole.

Here is a brief example of how to calculate effect sizes:

Name	Test 1	Test 2	Effect Size
Scooby Doo	514	602	1.508
Shaggy	571	703	2.001
Velma	614	674	1.097
Superman	622	684	0.850
Papa Smurf	474	587	1.549
Elsa	601	661	1.412
Peter Pan	485	479	0.164
Cinderella	657	761	1.426
Bam Bam	662	711	1.014
Fred Flintstone	575	645	1.138
Average	577.50	666.20	
Standard Deviation	67.23	78.67	
Average Standard Deviation	72.95		
Effect Size	1.22		

This is 1/3 of the students who were part of the sample size of the implementation of Mastery-Based Learning in Mathematics. I used cartoon names to hide the true names of the learners. As you can see the effect size was amazing and once I added in our students with disabilities the effect size moved closer to 2.00.

Standard Deviation Calculator:

https://tinyurl.com/yd4pr4u4

Step 1: Create spreadsheet with two points in time of at least three months. Input test score 1 and test score 2.

Step 2: Compute the average of test 1 and test 2.

Step 3: Use the standard deviation link above and calculate the standard deviation for both test scores.

Step 4: Find the mean (average) of the two standard deviations.

Step 5: Calculate Effect Size (Test 2- Test 1) then divide by step 4 calculation. This will provide the standard deviation.

Step 6: To calculate for individual student follow same process just select Test 1 and Test 2 for each child.

I used this evidence as a catalyst for change as the control group's effect size was .48. That was still amazing but not close to the 1.97.

For more information on calculating effect sizes please reach out to me.

To Reach Principal Hunter:
www.masterybasedlearning.com
Facebook.com/principalhunterofficial.com
Email:principalJhunter@gmail.com
LinkedIn: www.linkedin.com/in/principalhunterofficial
Twitter: @principaljack

Q: Could you share a copy of the walkthrough form you currently use?

A: Absolutely. Here is a copy of a 5-minute walkthrough ELA form. If you are interested in a pdf form or other content areas please email me: principalJhunter@gmail.com. You may also use this link for a digital version: **https://tinyurl.com/y7etc24s**

Five-Minute Observation Form

School:	_____
Date:	_____
Time:	_____
Program and Level:	_____
Grouping Format:	_____
Number in Group:	_____
Group Performance Level:	_____

In the box next to each General Feature indicate +, -, or NA. Check the circle next to each observed area.

[ ] **Instructor models instructional tasks when appropriate.**

o   Demonstrates the task (e.g., uses metacognition)
o   Proceeds in step-by-step fashion
o   Limits language to demonstration of skill
o   Makes eye contact with students, speaks clearly while modeling skill

[ ] **Instructor provides explicit instruction.**

o   Sets the purpose for the instruction
o   Identifies the important details of the concept being taught
o   Provides instructions that have only one interpretation
o   Makes connection to previously-learned material

[ ] Instructor engages students in meaningful interactions with language during lesson.

o   Provides and elicits background information
o   Emphasizes distinctive features of new concepts
o   Uses visuals and manipulatives to teach content as necessary
o   Makes relationships among concepts overt
o   Engages students in discourse around new concepts
o   Elaborates on student responses

[ ] Instructor provides multiple opportunities for students to practice instructional tasks.

o   Provides more than one opportunity to practice each new skill
o   Provides opportunities for practice after each step in instruction
o   Elicits group responses when feasible
o   Provides extra practice based on accuracy of student responses

Focus:	Phonemic Awareness [ ]	Phonics [ ]	Fluency [ ]
Vocabulary [ ]	Comprehension [ ]		

Comments:

Instructor: _____

☐ **Instructor provides corrective feedback after initial student responses.**
- ○ Provides affirmations for correct responses
- ○ Promptly corrects errors with provision of correct model
- ○ Limits corrective feedback language to the task at hand
- ○ Ensures mastery of all students before moving on

☐ **Instructor encourages student effort.**
- ○ Provides feedback during and after task completion
- ○ Provides specific feedback about student's accuracy and/or effort
- ○ Majority of feedback is positive
- ○ Celebrates or displays examples of student success in reading

☐ **Students are engaged in the lesson during teacher-led instruction.**
- ○ Gains student attention before initiating instruction
- ○ Paces lesson to maintain attention
- ○ Maintains close proximity to students
- ○ Transitions quickly between tasks
- ○ Intervenes with off-task students to maintain their focus

☐ **Students are engaged in the lesson during independent work.**
- ○ Independent work routines and procedures previously taught
- ○ Models task before allowing students to work independently
- ○ Checks for student understanding of the task(s)
- ○ Students use previously-learned strategies or routines when they come to a task they don't understand
- ○ Independent work is completed with high level of accuracy

☐ **Students are successful completing activities at a high criterion level of performance.**
- ○ Elicits a high percentage of accurate responses from group
- ○ Elicits a high percentage of accurate responses from individuals
- ○ Holds same standard of accuracy for high performers and low performers

Bibliography

1. Visible learning: a synthesis of over 800 meta-analyses relating to achievement Hattie - Routledge – 2010
2. Principles Dalio - Simon and Schuster – 2017
3. Visible learning for mathematics, grades K-12: what works best to optimize student learning Hattie et al. - Corwin Mathematics - 2017
4. Blended coaching: skills and strategies to support principal development Bloom - Corwin Press - 2006
5. Mindset: the new psychology of success Dweck - Random House - 2016
6. Brain Rules: 32 principles for surviving and thriving at work, home and school Medina - Pear Press - 2014
7. The credibility code: how to project confidence & competence when it matters most Alter - Meritus Books - 2012
8. Start with why: how great leaders inspire everyone to take action Sinek - Portfolio/Penguin – 2013
9. It's your ship: management techniques from the best damn ship in the navy Abrashoff - Warner Books - 2002
10. Failing forward: turning mistakes into stepping stones for success Maxwell - Thomas Nelson - 2007
11. Everyone communicates, few connect: what the most effective people do differently Maxwell - Thomas Nelson - 2010
12. Gung ho! Blanchard & Bowles - Morrow - 1998
13. This Is Day One: a Practical Guide to Leadership That Matters Dudley - Hachette Books - 2018
14. Good leaders ask great questions: your foundation for successful leadership Maxwell - Center Street – 2016
15. Becoming a reflective teacher Marzano & Boogren - Marzano Research Laboratory – 2012
16. Move your bus: an extraordinary new approach to accelerating success Clark - Touchstone - 2015
17. School leadership that works: from research to results Marzano et al. - Hawker Brownlow Education – 2006
18. The Conversation Club Stanley - Macmillan Publishing – 1990
19. It's about time: planning interventions and extensions in elementary school Buffum & Mattos - Solution Tree Press – 2015

Made in the USA
Monee, IL
27 December 2020

55736144R00098